NOBODY IS COMING TO SAVE YOU

NOBODY
IS COMING
TO SAVE
YOU

A GREEN BERET'S GUIDE
TO GETTING BIG SH*T DONE

LT. COL. SCOTT MANN, RET.

CENTER
STREET

NEW YORK NASHVILLE

Copyright © 2024 by David Scott Mann

Cover design by Kristen Paige Andrews. Cover copyright © 2024 by Hachette Book Group, Inc.

Center Street

Hachette Book Group

1290 Avenue of the Americas, New York, NY 10104

centerstreet.com

twitter.com/centerstreet

First Edition: October 2024

Center Street is a division of Hachette Book Group, Inc. The Center Street name and logo are registered trademarks of Hachette Book Group, Inc.

The publisher is not responsible for websites (or their content) that are not owned by the publisher.

The Hachette Speakers Bureau provides a wide range of authors for speaking events. To find out more, go to hachettespeakersbureau.com or email HachetteSpeakers@hbgusa.com.

Center Street books may be purchased in bulk for business, educational, or promotional use. For information, please contact your local bookseller or the Hachette Book Group Special Markets Department at special.markets@hbgusa.com.

Print book interior design by Sheryl Kober

Illustrations by Emma Brannon

Library of Congress Cataloging-in-Publication Data
Names: Mann, Scott, Lt Col., author.
Title: Nobody is coming to save you : a Green Beret's guide to getting big sh*t done / by Lt. Col. Scott Mann, Ret.
Description: First edition. | New York : Center Street, [2024]
Identifiers: LCCN 2024012037 | ISBN 9781546008286 (hardcover) | ISBN 9781546008330 (ebook)
Subjects: LCSH: Self-actualization (Psychology) | Leadership.
Classification: LCC BF637.S4 M33765 2024 | DDC 650.1—dc23/eng/20240515
LC record available at https://lccn.loc.gov/2024012037

ISBNs: 978-1-5460-0828-6 (hardcover), 978-1-5460-0833-0 (ebook)

Printed in the United States of America

LSC-C

Printing 1, 2024

To Monty:
None of this happens without you.
None of it.
What a ride it's been.
You are my world and I love you forever!

CONTENTS

Contents

CONCLUSION:

BLURB+

BY MIKE ROWE

When Scott Mann asked me to write the foreword for his latest book, I told him I'd love to, but that there simply wasn't time. I was in the middle of shooting a movie, running a foundation, writing my own book, and recording a televised version of my podcast.

"I completely understand," Scott said, "but I had to ask. Our nation's combat veterans respect you a great deal, and a quick shout-out from you would mean the world to them and to me."

"Well, that's different," I said. "A quick shout-out is easy. Like a blurb, right?"

"Yes! A blurb would be great!" said Scott. "Maybe just a few words on the back cover about the power of storytelling?"

"No problem," I said. "I'll get you something tomorrow."

"And maybe your take on the state of leadership in America and your views on where our leaders are falling short?"

"Well, that's a big topic, but sure, I can certainly say a few words on the importance of leading by example."

"That would be great," said Scott. "And maybe a few thoughts on the importance of living outside your comfort zone and the simple fact that anyone who embraces the power of their own story is capable of getting some big shit done—even in these divided times? Maybe something like that?"

Scott was smiling and nodding as he spoke to me, as was his lovely wife, Monty, who had just watched the two of us record another podcast episode in my Santa Monica studio.

"Are you sure you know what a blurb is?" I asked.

Scott smiled warmly and put his hand on my shoulder.

"Don't think of it as a blurb, Mike. Think of it as a blurb+!"

That's how Scott Mann persuaded me to read a book I didn't have time to read and then write a foreword that isn't a foreword, even though it lives in the front of the book. I suppose I shouldn't be surprised. Scott Mann has been using language in creative ways to persuade all sorts of people to do all sorts of things for a very long time. In the early days of the war, on the rooftops of Afghanistan, he persuaded countless Afghan civilians to put their confidence and trust in him, as he and his Green Beret teams taught them how to defend their villages from the Taliban. As he told me in our first interview, "Green Berets are very good at fighting. Modesty aside, there's no one better. But our real job over there wasn't kicking ass—it was winning the trust of Afghan people. And that's much easier said than done."

Indeed. At the end of the war, during that disastrous and

despicable withdrawal during which we abandoned hundreds of loyal Afghans who had fought bravely alongside American forces, Scott persuaded a small group of retired Americans to help him organize one last mission—an ingenious underground railroad that saved hundreds of Afghans from certain death at the hands of the Taliban. That endeavor was called Task Force Pineapple, which he later turned into a bestseller called *Operation Pineapple Express*—another book that you should read as soon as you're finished with this one.

(Quick sidebar on *Operation Pineapple Express*: That was Scott's first book. He'd never written a book before but refused to hire a ghostwriter. Which meant he had to persuade a major publisher to print his own story, in his own words. Also easier said than done.)

After that, Scott decided to write a play about the challenges of reentering civilian life after years on the battlefield. The play was called *Last Out,* a gut-wrenching, deeply personal, and utterly compelling look at the many sacrifices that come with serving your country. Scott had never written a play before, but of course, that didn't stop him. He also had zero experience as an actor, but that didn't stop him from casting himself in the lead role. The reaction was extraordinary: sold-out houses, rave reviews, and hundreds of veterans flocking to see the show, then staying for hours after the performance to share their personal stories with Scott. Then, somehow, Scott persuaded the Gary Sinise Foundation to subsidize a national tour of *Last Out,* the success of which has since been turned into a film, which you should also watch with all due speed.

(Quick sidebar on *Last Out:* I don't know exactly what Scott said to persuade Gary Sinise to finance a play written by a playwright with zero experience, with a lead actor who had never been onstage before, but I suspect it involved the incredible amount of healing that was going on after every performance. Given Gary's commitment to veterans, I also suspect that at some point, Scott Mann smiled, put his hand on Gary's shoulder, and said, "Don't think of it as a play, Gary. Think of it as a *play*+!")

I mention these various forays because the book you're about to read, *Nobody Is Coming to Save You: A Green Beret's Guide to Getting Big Sh*t Done,* might appear, at a glance, to be one more example of how this retired Green Beret can't seem to stay in his lane. I mean, what are we to make of a career soldier who woke up one day and decided to be an author, and then a playwright, and then an actor, and then a filmmaker, and now a career coach, motivational speaker, and full-time storyteller? Is this guy really capable of persuading the average citizen to connect more deeply with others? Can this former lieutenant colonel use just the right language to motivate a nation of hopelessly divided civilians to seize control of their own narrative and come together to get big shit done?

You bet your ass he can. And if this were an actual foreword, I'd tell you exactly how this book will accomplish that very thing. But since this is only a blurb+, I'll leave you with this:

I've grown weary of the specialist. The over-credentialed. The absolutist. Those certain-sounding dilettantes with no actual life experience, doling out advice as though it's their duty to give it and our great privilege to take it. If I'm going to consider life advice from anyone, especially in this day and age, I want to hear it from a generalist. Someone who has actually lived life "all the way up," as Hemingway said. Someone with no discernible lane from which to wander. Someone who has reinvented themselves time and time again. Someone who risked everything—and I mean everything—for a cause larger than themselves before daring to suggest the world might have something to learn from them. Someone who can talk me into writing a foreword that I didn't have time to write for a book I had no time to read—until I did.

Which is a long way of saying: Turn the page and let Scott Mann unlock the most important story you will ever hear. A story that needs to be told.

No, not *his.*

Yours.

Who This Book Is For,
and Why I'm Writing It

If you're reading this, you're likely standing in a bookshop or library or conference room wondering if—or even why—you might want to read a "self-help/leadership" book written by a retired US Army Green Beret. There is a tension in this formulation: Green Berets, so far as they're understood (and they are not understood well, if you ask me), are not generally thought of as touchy-feely types who would be just as happy discussing meaning, storytelling, emotional capital, modern life, social science, and the intentional application of good faith as they would be telling war stories. But it's true. I like talking about all of it. More than that, I feel the complete and total *need* to talk about all of it. For better or worse, it's become my obsession.

Hence, this book.

To be clear, these pages contain all the above: war stories, as well as discussions of feelings, modernity, and what it means to be human. More to the point, it's about what it means to be a human in our increasingly disorienting era. Right now, trust feels like it's at an all-time low, and the stakes feel like they are at an all-time high (or close to it). As I write, our country is bracing for another grueling presidential election; two intractable and complex wars are raging overseas; we are firmly in the era of mis- and disinformation; our lives are increasingly entangled with our digital devices and the worlds contained therein; artificial intelligence is ascendant with unknown consequences; our leaders in corporate, governmental, and even military organizations are busy telling us why they can't do things; inflation is high; remote work has become the norm; the COVID pandemic has altered our lives and negatively impacted learning for children everywhere; and powerful people in politics and the media are sowing division like their lives depend on it. And this is just a partial list of the many challenges we face as we fight day in and day out to navigate the world.

Ultimately, that's what this book is: a practical guide for any beleaguered, worn-down person who is desperate to break through the walls—real and imagined—that surround us. This book is for people who are tired of being lied to by our leaders. It's for the woman who craves someone to trust. It's for the businessperson who feels disconnected from others and the world around them. It's for the employee who feels distracted and beholden to his phone or computer, his calendar, his LinkedIn, his Slack channel. It's for the veteran who is depressed but doesn't know why. It's for the parent who feels defeated by forces they weren't even aware they were fighting in the first place. It's for the exhausted majority of Americans who are weary of the division and who know in their hearts that we have more in common than not.[1] It's for anyone who wants to do something about all of it.

It's for people who want to get shit done when the odds seem stacked against them.

(A little secret: That can work in your favor.)

Which brings us back to Green Berets.

The first time I saw a Green Beret was at Harrell's Soda Shop in Mount Ida, Arkansas, about ninety miles west of Little Rock. Mount Ida is my hometown: a tiny logging town, less than two square miles, home to about a thousand people. I knew damn near all of them.

Harrell's was an old-time soda fountain with a long counter and round tables. I'd walk there with friends after school or before ball games to scarf down hot dogs and nachos with a milkshake chaser. One day, when I was fourteen, the owner's son, Mark, walked in. He wore a Green Beret dress uniform pressed stiff as cardboard, brass buttons big and gleaming, black polished boots on his feet. He had a lanyard over his right shoulder, a Special Forces tab on his left, and his beret tipped perfectly over his right temple.

Every head in Harrell's swung to look at Mark, like he was the sheriff strolling in through saloon doors. He looked cool as hell, but that wasn't what hooked me. It was that he belonged to something called "Special Forces." They were also called "Green Berets." He was elite. And as a scrawny runt who struggled to fit in, I was as far from elite as you could get.

Right away, I wanted to know what a Green Beret was. Knees wobbling, ignoring the snickers of kids sitting behind me, I walked up to Mark, said hello, and asked him to tell me what all of this was all about. He smiled and ushered me to a nearby booth.

"Scott, Army Rangers, Navy SEALS, and other elite units are some of the best in the world at rolling in on a target and taking them down within minutes. They usually do the mission alone. What the Green Berets do is different. We work by, with, and through local people to help them stand up on their own. Ever since World War II, there have been these complex situations where you have to drop in a small team of specially trained advisors. That's us. We parachute in—"

"Cool!" I said, unable to contain myself.

He laughed. "Yeah. We parachute in and walk into the chaos. We connect at exactly the right spot, with precisely the right person. It might be a village elder or a tribal chief. Then, we get surrounded on purpose."

He could tell I didn't fully get it, so he kept explaining. "What I mean is, Green Berets learn the language, the culture, and the environment. Rather than roll in and roll out, we stay, and we stay, and we stay until the time is just right. Then we help the little guy stand up against the big guy. From the bottom up."

I was floored. I knew what I wanted to do with my life. In my mind, I already was a Green Beret. But my puny body had other ideas. The training pathway was intense. I failed multiple courses, many times. With each failure, I fought through the imposter syndrome and self-sabotage I'd developed from years of being bullied.

Fourteen years later, my dream had come true. For the rest of my Army career, I deployed with my fellow Green Berets to high-stakes, low-trust countries where I lived and fought alongside indigenous people, teaching them to stand up on their own. Often, we were far from reinforcements or resupply. If we got into trouble, there was nobody else coming to save us. It was just us. But "just us" resulted in damn good odds every time.

Green Berets excel at many things, but mostly we excel at getting shit done. This book is for people who want to get shit done. I wrote it for you, no matter where or who you are. Shit needs to get done. Good shit. Little shit. Big shit.

And it might as well be you who does it.

Come on, I'll show you how.

NOBODY IS COMING TO SAVE YOU

The wonderful boon of imagination we were given 35,000 years ago, as well as creating what is great in our culture, has also created an environment that seems out of control. We have the means to magnify our greed and have made a world that whirls around us so fast in such disturbing ways, that we can no longer trust our culture to reliably provide the psychological nourishment for us to develop fully as human beings.

—Joe Griffin and Ivan Tyrrell, eds.,
An Idea in Practice: Using the Human Givens Approach

CHAPTER 1

The Churn

We are dividing into hostile tribes cheering against each other, fueled by emotion and a mutual disdain that jeopardizes our future, instead of rediscovering our common ground and finding solutions.

—former secretary of defense James Mattis

I'm from the Government. How Ya Like Me So Far?

Let me tell you another story.

My chopper set down in the landing zone just outside the village. I hopped out, ducking under the rotor wash, my ruck slung over my shoulder, and walked over to meet the waiting team of Green Berets. We were in Kandahar Province, south-central Afghanistan. It was the spring of 2010. I'd deployed to Afghanistan for multiple tours, but the raw beauty of the place always staggered me. It was like landing in New Mexico or Arizona—open space for miles, rugged peaks in the near distance, the harshness, the emptiness. The poppies weren't yet blooming, but they would soon. The fields surrounded a village that was nestled in a fertile stretch of farmland we called the "green zone"—not to be confused with the Green Zone in Baghdad, Iraq, a fortress of compounds dedicated to security.

This place was anything but secure.

We approached the village on foot. From a distance, it looked almost quaint. A cluster of earthen buildings and crisscrossing dirt paths, home to fewer than a thousand residents. Goats and sheep grazed the rough edges of the town, and an encampment of nomadic Kuchi herders mulled among their herds. The Kuchi people complemented the landscape in their traditional, bright-colored clothing, sometimes embroidered with tiny mirrors that flashed the bright sunlight here and there.

The chopper lifted off. The Kuchi herders hustled into their tents. We kept walking.

We weren't there for the fresh air or the pristine landscape. The village was strategically important for the war against America's enemies. This was a Taliban safe haven, a rugged land dotted by hidden insurgent redoubts. In the surrounding countryside, Talib fighters would rest, regroup, train, and prepare for strikes against Kandahar, just a few dozen kilometers to the south, and even Kabul, around 250 kilometers away.

Our most urgent mission was not to use the village as a staging ground for raids against the Taliban, but to connect with the village and bring them around to our side. The people here were isolated and tribal; they were naturally sympathetic to the Taliban and their hard-line Islamist worldview, even if the Taliban didn't have their interests at heart. To save American lives, reduce the Taliban's reach into Afghanistan's cities, and secure this little village and their way of life, that needed to change.

As we entered the village—I'll call it Sarawa, a name I'm making up to protect real people in a real village that still exists today—it became less picturesque. The scars of endless war came into focus. Nearly every house had a fortified wall peppered with bullet holes. Mortars and rockets had destroyed many of the buildings, and only a handful of merchants still sold rugs, vegetables, or cheap electronics in the bombed-out bazaar at the town's center. As we walked to our walled compound, the streets were almost empty. When we greeted the few villagers we saw, they met our gaze with empty stares, their eyes revealing nothing other than their wordless desire for us to leave them alone.

The trajectory of the war was in flux in 2010. For nearly a decade, the posture of US and NATO forces toward Afghans had been one of assumed hostility. We thought that the only way to root out the Taliban was to treat every Afghan as a potential threat or a Taliban sympathizer. The tool our fighters carried was a hammer, and every Afghan was a nail.

During these years, a pattern had emerged. US forces would hole up in firebases and keep Afghans at arm's length during the day, then kick down doors at night, dragging sons, fathers, and grandfathers out of their beds to be interrogated, perhaps imprisoned. Meanwhile, the Taliban were going through neighborhoods, nailing threatening notes—messages we called "night letters"—to the doors of people they believed to be American collaborators. Sometimes they would beat and maim these suspected sympathizers in front of their neighbors, intimidating whole communities into submission.

The Afghan villagers, the people who would be truly decisive in this conflict, were being manipulated by all sides and left thrashing about in this churn of tension and conflict.

As the war dragged on, the Special Forces community became aware of this loss of social capital and decided to get back to its roots: We would immerse ourselves more deeply in at-risk Afghan communities. We had been living in walled compounds for years, always keeping the local populace at bay. Now we faced a need to connect more effectively with people who were disconnected from each other, and from us. It wouldn't be easy to suddenly ask for a sit-down with village leaders and say, "We're from the government, how do you like us so far? Mind if we live here?"

This is what we were doing in Sarawa.

From the moment we arrived, we made three promises. One, if they didn't want us there, now or at any time in the future, then just say so and we'd leave. Two, if they allowed us to stay, things in the village would get harder before they got easier. The Taliban were going to continue to come for them and their families and for us Americans. But three: When they do come, us Green Berets are going to climb up our ladders, take positions on the rooftops, and we're going to fight. We're going to do this whether you villagers join us or not.

We were allowed to stay and set up our camp in a couple of rented buildings on the edge of town. This didn't mean we were embraced, however. The village was a classic low-trust, high-stakes environment. How could it not be? Like so many other Afghan towns, Sarawa had been through forty years of nonstop war. No children played in the streets. Everyone in the little community had post-traumatic stress. During the day, villagers shuffled around in a trancelike state. It's called *inescapable shock*, a fear-based, hypnotic condition where a person is stuck between fight and flight.

The people of Sarawa were caught in a constant churn of *distraction*. Occupiers came and went. NATO forces rotated home every year. Uncertainty hung in the air like a fog.

They were in a constant churn of *disengagement*. They lacked any sense of purpose in themselves and in their community. Years of conflict had robbed them of their why.

Villagers were in a constant churn of *disconnection*. They didn't trust each other. They didn't trust their government.

And they sure as hell didn't trust us. But it was their trust that us Green Berets needed more than anything.

We had a remarkable team in that village. Their main mission was establishing human connection. There was Captain Mike and his warrant officer, David, who met regularly with elders from two rival tribes, trying to persuade them to set their differences aside.

There was Craig, the senior engineer sergeant, who helped install and repair a communal well. Like in all desert climates, water was life, and if we lost access to that water, it would mean losing support in the village. There was Billy, the senior medical sergeant, who examined two young boys complaining of stomach pain. Their grandfather was the most influential tribal elder in the entire province.

There was Tracy, the senior communications sergeant, who stayed in the command hooch, working the radio in his giant headphones like a LaGuardia air traffic controller. He would process all the intelligence reports that flowed in, building a picture for that night's impending Taliban attack.

There was Justin, the senior weapons sergeant, who went out and inspected the town's limited arsenal. He oiled beat-up AK-47s and reassembled colonial-era British Enfield rifles, bolt-action long guns the farmers and shepherds carried into the fields.

The duties of these men were workaday, but there was nothing casual about what they did. Every time they made a move, they were vulnerable. Every scrap of food they ate had to be airdropped by plane, and all of them probably lost twenty-five pounds or more over the course of six months. A daytime trip to the bazaar for fresh vegetables or local meat often attracted incoming fire. Any excursion beyond the gate, no matter how close, always brought the rattle of enemy AKs. The men habitually circled up and joined hands before undertaking any task outside the wire, to say their peace, because they knew any day could be their last.

The nights were worse. As soon as darkness fell, the Taliban attacked with heavy weapons, just like they had the night before, and every night before that.

While these men—our men—lived in Sarawa, and other tough villages, I came and went. As an architect of this Village Stability Operation, part of my job was to find out what they needed and get it to them. Sometimes that meant pounding on metal trailers on large bases to find a hydrologist or a farming expert to help our team gain rapport with aloof villagers. Other times it meant securing funding by accompanying skeptical generals in crisp uniforms fresh from Washington, explaining how this work helped the war effort. Sometimes I'd chaperone nervous congressional delegations in chest armor and blast helmets, men and women who hurried in and only stayed long enough to be able to tell their constituents they had seen up close what it was we were fighting for.

In essence, my job was storyteller. I served as a strategic connector between this team of Green Berets and the larger world outside Afghanistan. I explained, through showing and telling, the incredible work this team—and dozens of other teams like them—was doing, and why it was so crucial to America's policy goals. I led guided discussions with tribal elders, development experts, and diplomats, all of whom lacked trust in one another, to say nothing of Afghans in general.

I bridged these divides by telling them about what went on every night in Sarawa.

Whatever our daytime duties—running back and forth to Kandahar for more supplies, digging an irrigation ditch, pulling an infected tooth, helping with a harvest of summer wheat—we fought at night. We might have been exhausted, we might have been met with blank stares throughout the day, but every night we fought. The villagers we helped throughout the day wouldn't show, but that didn't matter. We fought.

Whenever an attack came, we rolled out of our cots, pulled on whatever kit was nearby, and scurried up to the roof with our rifles, often barefoot or shirtless. Every time we fought, we hoped the farmers would race up to their rooftops as well and begin firing their AKs at the same targets we were firing on. But even if they didn't, we kept hoping. Maybe, one night, they would take up arms and join us. We didn't know if they would. But we had hope. The team would remain there even if they were the only ones on the rooftop.

Attacks came and went. Automatic weapons cracked in the darkness. Sometimes rockets streaked toward our compound from the shadows. Hour after hour, we returned fire, staring down our muzzles looking for movement. The Taliban wanted Sarawa, and these teammates weren't going to let them take it. Sometimes, shots came from within the village. We never shot back if the fire was ineffective. We couldn't risk hurting an innocent villager. Our tracer bullets drew green phosphorescent slashes across the night air. Above us, the Milky Way was so bright that every star in the galaxy seemed to spill down onto our heads. It was beautiful. It was hell.

We fought from the rooftops all night long. When the sun rose, the Taliban melted back into the countryside, almost like they were made of rock or dust. The team hobbled down the ladders, exhausted, carrying our wounded and sometimes our dead. When the sun set, the whole terrible tableau repeated itself. The gunfire crackled back to life; the Afghans stayed down below in the safety of their homes. We went up the ladders. We knew this was where we had to be. Up high. Above the churn. We had to show reluctant Afghan farmers how to rise above their fear.

Then one night, under attack on the rooftop, we heard it.

Off to one side, a rifle shot. A muzzle flash. Shooting in the same direction as our team.

Not from our rooftop. From the rooftop of one of the villagers.

A nearby farmer had made a decision. Probably terrified, definitely unsure of what it would mean to the rest of the villagers, he had nonetheless slung his rifle over his shoulder, climbed onto his roof, and joined the Green Berets in defending Sarawa. Who knows when we got through to him, when we connected? Who knows what precipitated this connection? Was it when we helped till a field? When we gave a few stitches to a boy who'd cut himself climbing fences? Was it when we resolved a family land dispute?

We would never know, and this night we didn't care.

We continued firing, now with new resolve. Tomorrow night, there would be one more Afghan, and another the night after that, and so on until every farmer and shop owner in the village was on their roof, fighting alongside us.

Standing up for themselves. The way they were meant to. The way Green Berets were meant to assist them.

By leading from the rooftop.

Know Thine Enemy

That story is the inspiration for and distillation of Rooftop Leadership, a concept for strategic influence I developed in chaos that is defined by human connection.* For the past thirty years, establishing and nurturing human connections has been

---

*If you want a deeper explanation of Rooftop Leadership, you can watch my TED Talk at https://youtu.be/M78sDuehUnk?si=OW80q4uphhYXl4eO.

my purpose. Lately, it's been my obsession. My work has taught me how and why people can connect, and more than that, why they *need* to connect. Nobody was coming to save us. We couldn't fight the Taliban without the help of the people of Sarawa. To achieve that, we needed to figure out how to inspire reluctant, disconnected people to join us on the rooftop.

This need is in no way unique to Green Berets or our mission any more than chaos is unique to Afghanistan. You find it in real estate, in sales, in human resources, in community organizing, in politics, in PTA meetings, in summer camps, on corporate outings. In our modern world, the ability to connect with others seems to be the rarest of skills and mobilizing them to action the scarcest of outcomes.

Which brings me to an essential component of my Rooftop Leadership mission: defining the enemy. In Afghanistan, the Taliban was the enemy. Even though that war was confusing, and it was sometimes difficult to tell who was Taliban and who wasn't, there was never any doubt about whom we were fighting.

But here at home, it's trickier.

Veterans often have a difficult time when they return home from war, and I was no different. I was floored by what I found after my time in the Army ended in 2013. Why were people so angry? Why were neighbors yelling at each other over small disputes? Why were Americans treating other Americans like they were mortal enemies? What was going on?

What I soon realized was that, like Afghanistan, our own country, communities, and businesses were also at a low-trust, high-stakes inflection point. As I looked around, I began to recognize the *real* enemy. Just like in Sarawa and many other Afghan villages, people everywhere were (and still very much are) grappling with this enemy.

What is it? An insidious, resourceful, and unstoppable beast I call the Churn.

Feel the Churn

"What the hell?" Mark typed *Randy Atkins* into the search bar of his Facebook page one more time and hit enter.

Nothing.

It was as if Randy had disappeared.

Mark stared at his screen, blinking in confusion. He'd been blocked! By a man he'd known for nearly thirty years! Mark flipped over to Instagram and searched there too. Nothing. Randy was gone.

"I don't believe this," he pronounced to an empty room, trying to reconstruct what had happened.

The thing that started it was a repurposed meme of "shitty masks throughout history" Mark had posted. It included a picture of a lady wearing a rubber horse head, a guy wearing a fishbowl giving a thumbs-up, and of course someone wearing a COVID surgical mask. You get the idea. Mark was trying to be lighthearted about a serious issue, and most of the responses reflected that—but not Randy's.

"You don't believe in wearing a mask?" Randy had messaged.

At first, Mark thought Randy was kidding. Only a few weeks earlier, Randy had posted a similar meme on his own Facebook page, and now Mark was following suit, putting a silly spin on his frustrations with living in the time of COVID.

Mark waited a few hours before sending Randy a private message of a photo of a beaming guy with his head in a cardboard box, the face cut out. The caption read, "This is my mask."

And that's when Randy disappeared. Mark had been unfriended. He'd been blocked. He'd been canceled.

This had to be some kind of joke. These two men had worked together in the music business for three decades; they knew each other's families; they spent holidays together; they hung out for no reason.

Mark called Randy. No answer.

He called again and again, leaving multiple voicemail messages. No response.

Mark texted, apologizing that he'd offended his friend.

Crickets.

Mark, who is also a friend of mine, recounted this over lunch one day not too long after the incident. "I just don't know how this happened, Scott. I mean, I've always had a dry sense of humor. I can be a smart-ass even, you know that. Randy knows that too. But to block me? I don't know what to do. I've tried to apologize, but he won't respond. I guess I'll have to move on. That's just how it is these days."

That's just how it is.

Ask yourself: How many scary, stressful, or uncomfortable situations do we face nowadays? Pandemics. Recessions. Elections. Layoffs. Mergers. Bonuses. Everything is elevated, all the time. The stakes always feel high, and this makes people intolerant, irritable, uncreative, critical. Our more nuanced perceptions are numbed. Our fine motor skills are stunted. We lose a sense of perspective. We shut down. Look around. We know something is wrong, but we don't know what it is exactly and we sure as shit don't know what to do about it.

Welcome to the modern world.

Welcome to the Churn.

What Is the Churn?

The Churn is volatile. If you charted it, it would look like an EKG.

The Churn is divisive. It creates in-groups and out-groups that don't talk to each other but rather past each other.

The Churn is fear-inducing. When we are afraid, we focus more on surviving than thriving.

The Churn breeds uncertainty. As soon as we feel as though we have a handle on a problem, something new and unexpected appears, leaving us feeling unprepared and constantly off-balance.

The Churn is complex. It presents us with *wicked problems* whose solutions are nonlinear and require framing by diverse groups that are often at odds.

The Churn is crowded. When you're in it, it's harder to both listen and be heard.

The Churn is ambiguous. When you're in the Churn, it's nearly impossible to see the full picture.

The Churn erodes confidence. Not just in each other, but in institutions, businesses, nonprofits, families. It even erodes confidence in ourselves.

The Churn loathes nuance. It's not interested in detailed arguments. It wants bluntness and self-righteousness.

The Churn doesn't care for facts. It prefers opinions fueled by fear and anger.

The Churn loves interruptions. It lives off pulling you one way and then the next, often multiple times per minute.

The Churn thrives online. All of the Churn's challenges are exacerbated when encountered in the digital worlds in which we spend more and more time.

The Churn is relentless. It never stops, even when you get out of it. And it's not going to stop, either. It is impossible to kill.

These are not reasons to despair. The Churn wants you to despair.

Do not let it.

The Four Ds

The Churn's main components are what I call "the Four Ds." These are:

Distraction

I recently attended a conference in Washington, DC, where I'd been hired to consult with senior executives. As it kicked off, a company president took the stage and began flicking through a PowerPoint presentation. By slide three, every subordinate leader within my direct line of sight was on their phone.

According to psychologist Dr. Gloria Mark,[2] the average attention span for an adult human has dropped from two and a half minutes in 2004 to just forty-seven seconds in 2023. It's continuing to decline. Neuroscientist Sahar Yousef says, "Smartphones are the biggest drains on the human brain in the twenty-first century."[3] We look up from our phones, we look down, we tap a button to like, we scroll, we repeat. All of these actions shoot a tiny surge of dopamine through our system. For a brief moment, we feel connected, but then the feeling is gone and the emptiness returns. So we repeat: We move on to the next TikTok video, the next online comment, the next Instagram story. Multitasking is a myth for our ancient brains. Every time we switch focus, there is a loss in brain energy. All of this contributes to our...

Disengagement

The Great Resignation. The Talent Tsunami. Quiet quitting. Gallup reports that 68 percent of employees are disengaged at work.[4] Right now, people lack purpose. Whether you work in health care or for the US Navy, when you start to lose purpose bad things happen. Humans need purpose, we are meaning-seeking creatures. Without meaning, isolation creeps in, which leads directly to...

Disconnection

Our mechanistic, consumer-based mass technologies have driven a wedge between people everywhere. They have interrupted and short-circuited our ability to connect with one another, the natural world, and ourselves.

Disconnection erodes the foundations of family and community. It compromises the social capital that binds us together. This causes society to fracture in a range of ways. Disconnection causes veterans to feel like strangers in their own country. It causes a spike in mental health issues. It prevents parents from being able to talk to their children. It keeps leaders from articulating shared goals and visions. It quite literally breeds madness. All of this leads to...

Distrust

Most social scientists agree that successful liberal democracies rely on three basic ingredients:

1. Trust in our institutions;
2. Trust in each other;
3. Myths that bind us together.

How do you think we're doing?

Yeah, not great.

Poll after poll shows that a majority of Americans have lost trust in our politicians, our government, our media, even our military. According to one study, 75 percent of Americans have lost trust in the federal government and 68 percent have lost trust in one another.[5] Think about how these trends show up during elections, in your office, at Little League games, at a family reunion.

Alternatively, think about how they show up in *your mind*.

The Trance

The early afternoon sun was still high over the mountains when I piled my paper plate with fried chicken and found a seat at a table at my family reunion. About forty-five family members showed up that July Fourth in 2013 at a retreat in the North Carolina mountains.

We had been holding annual reunions here since the mid-1980s, but this year it felt even more important to come together. Since I'd retired from the Army, the country I'd served felt tense and angry and distrustful. No matter where I went, there it was. I saw road rage every time I got in the car. I couldn't watch cable news, with partisans screaming talking points at each other. Politics had become shrill and nasty and petty. It felt like everyone in the country was at war, fighting amongst ourselves.

The retreat took place around a 1920s-era house made of hand-hewn lumber that sat on a hilltop overlooking a long grassy slope that ran down to a ball field on the bank of the Laurel River. The building had a huge kitchen perfect for feeding multiple generations of our hungry family. The barbecue was going, and relatives had brought trays piled with fresh-sliced tomatoes and vegetables from their gardens. Red, white, and blue tablecloths covered the picnic tables. Over the door, someone had hung the official banner of the party: an American flag we handed down through the years, signed by each reunion's host.

As I dug into my pile of chicken, I sat with an older man I had known since childhood. I'll call him Rob. He had thinning white hair and a gentle smile. He was one of the kindest men I knew—I had never once heard him speak ill of anyone.

After eating, we pushed aside our plates and caught up. At first, he told me about some other mutual family friends. But then he got very quiet. Apparently, the son in one of these families supported a politician he hated. I don't remember which politician—Republican or Democrat—but it didn't matter. What I do remember was the change that came over Rob. As he talked about the son, his brow furrowed, and he pursed his lips. "Disgusting," he said, spitting on the ground.

I was stunned. Before my eyes, this elderly family friend had transformed from the kind, generous man I knew into an angry partisan. Rob's entire demeanor had changed. He was now irritated and aggressive, as if poised to attack.

I had seen this look many times, most recently in Afghanistan. It was a primal look, the kind shared by warring clans. It was the look of the enemy across the barricades.

Rob couldn't perceive my shock; he was too caught up in anger. He kept talking about the boy's politics. He spat again. His voice dripped with disdain. It was as if something hidden from view had suddenly become visible.

Rob's mind had been hijacked. He was in a trance.

A trance brought on by the Churn.

My Promise to You

The enemy was not Rob, and it wasn't this kid he used to love. The enemy is not the partner sitting across from you. The enemy is not the politician you hate. The enemy isn't the guy who cut you off on the drive home. The enemy isn't the old friend who unfriended you on Facebook.

The enemy is the Churn.

So, what to do? To stay in the Churn is to remain entranced. You will thrash about, feeling frustrated and stuck. You will care only about survival.

But it doesn't have to be this way. The world shouldn't be deprived of your potential just because our human terrain and social conditions have changed under our feet. There is a better way. I promise.

Yeah, yeah. Most promises made in self-help books are bullshit. You know it, I know it. But this isn't bullshit. I have no patience for theory. These are tangible, hard-earned lessons, from some of the most low-trust places on earth.

I promise that if you dig into this book, you're going to see human nature differently. This includes your own nature. I ran a lot of crazy miles to find this approach. I have failed a ton. But on my journey, I've discovered a relevant way to think about the challenges we each face. We're going to learn how to step out of the Churn and how to lead from the bottom up. We'll share a grammar for the wicked problems around human nature and human connection we see right in front of us but don't know how to address. We'll emerge with tools for talking to ourselves in times of self-sabotage and doubt. We'll learn to build bridges over and around the Churn to mobilize others to action. We will learn how to own any room we walk into, not in the sleazy transactional sales pitch way, but in an authentic way that leads to relatability and relevance.

Ultimately, this is how we get big shit done: by being able to relate to the pain of others, and by being more relevant to their goals.

This is what people follow, especially when they are scared, angry, and entranced by our common enemy, the Churn.

Now What?

If you're still reading, you've likely located yourself within the Churn and are committed to doing something about it. Maybe you want to get out of it. Maybe you simply would like to feel better about yourself and those around you. Maybe you want to get shit done, big or small.

Great. But how?

We're almost to the "practical guide" portion of this book. Here's how it'll go.

First, we're going to get *below the waterline* of human nature. We'll recognize that we are, despite a few hundred years of modernity, still primal creatures ruled fundamentally by hundreds of thousands of years of biological hardwiring. We'll learn to perceive the threats and the opportunities that our deep, biological selves perceive effortlessly but that are often invisible in our modern, mechanistic world. We'll also see what's at stake if we refuse our nature and reject community, neighborliness, and the natural world.

Next, we'll get into the nitty-gritty of Rooftop Leadership. Nobody wins alone. We may not always like each other, but we do always need each other. This requires human connection. And in order to connect in this Churn, we're going to get MESSSy (bear with me).

We're going to explore how **M**eaning is forged; delve into our **E**motions; mine our **S**ocial capital; refine our **S**torytelling chops; and talk about our **S**truggles.

While getting MESSSy, we'll learn to view our behavior and the behavior of others in a new light. We'll also learn how to wield authentic influence when dealing with (quite understandably) reluctant people, in places where leadership is in short supply.

Finally, we'll bring it all together so that you can focus on what you need to do, whether that's leading a company, writing a book, running for office, raising kids, chairing a school board, overseeing a home renovation, beginning a new career, or simply asking for help when you most need it.

Green Berets get shit done, and you will too. Let's get after it.

CHAPTER 2

The Human Operating System

The Closet, My .45

My wife, Monty, stormed out of the house.

"Fuck it," I spat as I stepped into our bedroom's walk-in closet and shut the door. This was the moment I had been waiting for.

It was quiet. Racks of clothing muffled the sound of my breath. Sweat ran down my face. I hadn't showered in days, I had week-old stubble, and I reeked.

It was dark, but I knew where I was going. I pushed past shirts, shoes, and rows of childhood trophies to the compartment where I kept my guns. I unlocked the safe's door. My hand closed around the grip of my .45. I pulled it out. Time stopped.

Mere months after retiring from the Army, my demons had come to life. I was disconnected. Isolated. Voiceless. Purposeless. The country I'd fought to defend for my entire adult life was riven by distrust and division. This was now 2015, a year after the protests and riots in Ferguson, Missouri, following the killing of Michael Brown by a local police officer. Wherever I looked, people were angry. I was disgusted at the way Americans were tearing each other apart while our institutional leaders seemed to do nothing. Worse, in some cases, they actually egged it on, as if sowing more division was somehow good for us. Or if not for us, then for their bottom line, however they defined that.

I looked around and couldn't see any good, no matter how much I squinted. The country was on fire.

Was this what I'd fought for, what my friends and teammates had died or suffered grievous injury for? I slid to the floor, gun still in hand. I was exhausted, depleted, depressed. I was having unpredictable mood swings, erupting into anger at the tiniest provocation. I never wanted to leave the house. When I walked into a room, our boys—twelve, fifteen, and seventeen—would tiptoe away. They never knew which version of Dad they were going to get.

When you added my general shittiness to a stable but by no means sufficient financial situation, you can easily understand why Monty had stormed out on me that day. She was the hero around our house, not me, Mr. Green Beret. She'd shouldered it all. For nearly two decades, she had sacrificed nonstop. She put her life on hold, raised our boys, and held the family together while I was deployed. Well, I was back now, but was I really? No. I was there physically, but mentally and spiritually I was a ghost—my self-worth was shot. I was spiraling into the void.

I have no recollection what our argument was about that day, not specifically. All I know is that we stomped away from each other with no resolution. And now there I was, in the closet, my .45 in hand.

Fuck this, I thought. *Fuck all of this. What's the point?! I am a burden. I'm causing pain to my wife and boys. If this is the man I will be for the rest of my life, then they'd be better off without me.*

I tilted the pistol back and pushed its muzzle into the base of my chin. My heart pounded; my breath slowed. The gun was heavy. It had a magazine in it. There was a round in the chamber. A line of weak light pressed through the crack at the base of the closet door. Sweat dripped off my nose. The world receded.

Suddenly, there were two more people in the closet. One hissed, *Just get it done. It's one more shitty task and then it'll be over. Don't be a fucking pussy.* The other voice said, *Are you kidding? This is how it's going to go? This is it? You're not gonna fight? You're being a fucking pussy.* Back and forth it went, like a grim cartoon playing out as I held the gun in my sweaty palm.

Then I heard the front door open, followed by voices. I could make out my middle son, Cooper, who'd come home from school with friends.

Shit, I thought. *My kid is going to hear a shot and find me in the closet with my brains all over the ceiling.*

I pulled the pistol from my chin and regarded it. I saw the grim steel, felt its heft. Suddenly, it was a white-hot foreign object burning my skin. I'd held a gun so many times that it was second nature, but now I felt a desperate urge to get it away from me. I felt the urge to vomit. Ashamed, I cleared the chamber, locked the pistol in the safe, and skulked out of the closet. I was unwilling to live, but unable to die.

All I knew was that, if it was going to work out, I was going to have to change.

But how?

Below the Waterline

In that moment, I had no idea how.

What I did have were my instincts. And my instincts were screaming just like they did when things got nasty in combat: *You've got to change, man. You've lost your connection to yourself. You've got to go deep. You've got to get a grip on who you are and what you're about. You've got to get a real and true understanding of your own personal human nature.*

You've got to get below the waterline.

Close your eyes and picture an iceberg. What do you see? I see a frozen blue-white mountain—sometimes a pyramid,

sometimes a wall—drifting almost motionlessly on a sheet of gray water. But what you perceive to be the iceberg, that visible portion above the waterline, is only 20 percent of the entire thing. The other 80 percent is under the water, invisible to us poor saps on the surface. But just because it's invisible doesn't make it less important. The part of the iceberg below the waterline is what sank the *Titanic*.

This iceberg is my metaphor for our current human operating system.

The tip of the iceberg, what's visible above the waterline, represents the modern component of our human operating system. It accounts for our actions in what I call *contract society*. This is the world in which we live, work, and play every day. It's all the stuff in plain sight. It's the realm of cash flow reports, sales meetings, COVID mitigation rules. It's Zoom fatigue, it's getting kids to soccer practice, it's binge-watching *Yellowstone*. It's the recession, inflation, supply chain issues. It's drinking, it's taking drugs. It's social media, it's elections, it's 24/7 news alerts. Its main currency is, well, currency—cold hard cash. It is the consumerist, material world. It isn't the Churn, but it is absolutely where the Churn lives and thrives.

The massive chunk below the waterline represents the more traditional component of our human operating system. It accounts for our actions in what I call *status society*.[6] This is the world ruled by our ancient, ingrained, evolutionary roots. It's the world of relationships, barter, customs, ritual. Many such societies still exist in the modern world. Take Afghanistan. Once you get off the paved Ring Road and into the countryside, one's position in civil society is based not on what one has but rather on the *status* one maintains within one's group.* Its main currency is a two-sided coin called honor and shame. The Churn still exists, but not to the same extreme. Here's why.

Social capital, the tangible and intangible links between humans in these rough places, is the oldest form of capital.

---

*Words matter. As a combat advisor, I'm well aware of many of the academic and cultural sensitivities around the words *tribe* and *tribal*. For the purpose of this book, I reverently employ these words interchangeably with *status*, *primal*, *clan*, and *traditional society* in order to convey our link to our ancient roots.

Relationships are at the core of group dynamics in status society. In fact, status societies are governed by leaders who don't necessarily inherit their right to lead. Rather, they have big relationship portfolios that enable them to engage multiple groups, to bring opportunities to their group, and to restore relationships when they are damaged, both between groups and within their own. Before money was brought into the world, there was an emphasis on reciprocity. "I'll do this for you because you did this for me."

We all know this isn't how it works in contract society, where the emphasis shifts from relationships to transactions. Money was invented to allow transactions to happen fluidly and at scale. It birthed new kinds of competition, the bottom line, the profit motive, and, at this late stage, fiduciary responsibility that puts shareholders at the center of all business concerns, sometimes (and sometimes often) at the expense of society at large.

In today's Churn, this transactional mindset is further exacerbated by the peculiarities of our "engagement and attention" economy. Everything is focused on a digital performance in a re-presented, virtual realm;[†] the result is that we can be

---

[†]The term *re-presented* (with hyphen) has a unique meaning here that is different from *represented* (without hyphen), which means "brought clearly before the mind." In this context, author Iain McGilchrist explains *re-presenting* as creating "a virtual world, a copy that exists in conceptual form in the mind." Throughout this book, I will use *re-present* as a way of describing the rise of a virtual world, as opposed to the natural world where we live, work, and play.

led to focus less on actual physical engagement.[7] We manage our personal brands on superficial playing fields, often at the expense of making broad, deep, and in-person connections with others.

As we'll soon learn, if we're going to deal successfully with the Churn, making these kinds of human connections is the name of the game.

To Get Without Getting Got

The iceberg's waterline is one way to think about how our human operating system is divided, sometimes against itself.

Another way is less metaphorical. It is, in fact, physiological.

Did you know that animals have divided, asymmetrical brains?[8] Humans included. This doesn't mean we have two brains. It's not right brain versus left brain, it's not either/or—it's both/and. It's how the halves interact with each other using a neural membrane called the corpus callosum, even though the halves are hardwired to have very different priorities.

Let me explain. Imagine a bird eating sunflower seeds in a park. The left hemisphere of the bird's brain is laser-focused on eating the seeds. It blocks out everything else. It manipulates its surroundings to grab and peck—to have the seed. The left hemisphere is obsessed with obtaining. It's so obsessed that in a very real sense, it *becomes* the seed. There is nothing else but the seed and the hunger it sates.[9]

Simultaneously, the bird's right hemisphere is focused on the bird's connections to its surroundings. It prioritizes the cat lurking on a nearby bench, the breeze in the tree boughs, the human being that might come too close for comfort. It is focused on its relationship with the external, natural world.

Dr. Iain McGilchrist, a psychiatrist, neuroscientist, and literary scholar whose work has had a profound influence on me, refers to the left hemisphere as the "Emissary," and the right hemisphere as the "Master." While the Emissary focuses on grabbing, acquiring, and manipulating its immediate environment, it remains subservient to the Master, which maintains constant connection to the natural world. Each hemisphere works simultaneously on very different things. They don't work at cross-purposes, but in tandem.

This arrangement allows the bird "to get without getting got," as McGilchrist so cleverly puts it.

Millions upon millions of years of evolution have led to this arrangement. It's a miracle, really. We can do one thing very well while never losing sight of our surroundings.

But our tech-heavy world has changed things, at least for us humans. According to McGilchrist, over the last hundred years or so, the left hemisphere of modern humans has become obsessively focused on its own dominance. It wants to be the Master. And its main tool for trying to achieve this is imitation.

Humans, with their active imaginations, tend to imitate other things. In societies where tracking and hunting are part of daily life, humans don animal pelts and imitate the animal they're stalking for food. It's the original theory of mind: If one can imitate an animal so completely, then you begin to think and act like it, making the task of hunting both easier and more meaningful.

McGilchrist maintains that this human penchant for imitation has migrated into our machine-dominated world. Modern humans have become rapidly entangled with our mechanized civil society, and as such, we have become consumed with imitating not animals, but machines themselves.

The machines we have designed are ruled by logic, algorithms, language, transaction, and control, all left-hemisphere brain functions. The re-presented virtual realm that we perceive and receive from our computers is also the domain of our left brain, which wants to imitate our machines and manipulate our surroundings. So, like machines, we have become more swayed by logic, by transaction, by control. It may be a stretch to say we live algorithmically, but anyone who has bumped into a signpost or a person while walking down the street and scrolling Instagram or TikTok will have to admit that they are at least being ruled by algorithms more than they were before the advent of the smartphone. At any rate, as our imitation of and entanglement with machines grows more pervasive, our left brain, hell-bent on manipulation and acquisition, begins to eclipse the dominance of the right brain, which is more concerned with context and connection.

For humans, context and connection lead directly to storytelling, empathy, and relationships. Across the full arc of our evolutionary history—before we could write, before we could make fire, before we could knap arrowheads or sew satchels—storytelling has been the prime foundation of human society.

The modern human's left brain wants you to forget that. It wants you to accept our re-presented digital realm as a thing that is actually real. It wants to put you in the Churn and it wants to keep you there. As this has happened more and more, our right brain has cast around, unsure of what to do as its long, pre-historical reliance on relationships and connections has faded into the darkness of the Churn.

Well-Dressed Neanderthals

Contract society, our above-the-waterline realm in which the Churn thrives and our left brain dominates, may feel all-encompassing, but it is relatively new. Officially, it came into existence around ten thousand years ago with the first agricultural revolution; but the truly modern world we are part of in Los Angeles, New York City, Atlanta, Little Rock, and so on is only about a hundred years old.

Status society, our below-the-waterline foundation where the Churn takes a backseat and the right brain is more in charge, has been around for a long, long time. It came into existence more or less the moment we "became" human around 250,000 years ago. In some sense, it sprang from our imaginations as we sat around the communal fire, telling the world and our place in it into existence with our songs, stories, and traditions.

While contract society may feel dominant, we originally all came from status societies. In other words, our ancient past is still with us. Our human legacy of being primal hunters, gatherers, and nomads is a quarter of a million years old, and that legacy still dominates our blood and DNA.

But don't take my word for it. According to Jared Diamond, the award-winning anthropologist and author, people are far more traditional than they are modern.[10] We are well-dressed Neanderthals.

A few years after my suicide scare, I had an epiphany: The above-the-waterline Churn seemed to dominate our behavior, but what's below the waterline—those ancient, hardwired neural pathways—are potentially far more influential. We simply don't realize it. The recent phenomenon of our left brain's desire to control our modern existence has blinded us to our primal inheritance. We're asleep at the switch.

Because of my service in rural Afghanistan, I was familiar with tribalism, but our modern-world version of tribalism felt different. It was darker. Shame. Vengeance. Feud. It was a shadow tribalism.* Our people here at home were so disconnected and so entranced that they didn't even clock their discord as primal—insidiously, they thought it was *modern*, and if they happened to regard it as a problem, then they mistakenly assumed the solution would also be a modern one.

Wrong.

And so here we are. Where one lifelong friend gets rejected by another because of a stupid mask meme, or where an elder disowns a younger member of his family over politics. Worst of all, our leaders, who are supposed to be stewards, who are supposed to build trust, share abundance, define our community, and adhere to the rule of law, are instead fomenting distrust, preaching scarcity, shattering community, and chucking rules and laws by the wayside. All because it benefits them personally. But remember—they are in the Churn too. Perhaps more than us regular folks who make up the exhausted majority.

(Note: We're not only exhausted because our divisionist leaders too often suck—we're also exhausted because of the Churn. Know thine enemy!)

---

*There are many desirable aspects of tribal society, even in modern times. Sebastian Junger makes a strong case about the primal sense of community and collective suffering in his book *Tribe*. However, there are also dark elements to our tribal roots around feud, shame, and vengeance that we seem to embrace in our disconnected, trance state without the balance of more favorable tribal aspects of community, atonement, and restoration for the greater good.

Our tech-soaked hubris causes us to believe we have evolved beyond our status society nature. But we haven't. We're just as primal as we were ten thousand years ago. Perhaps we're even worse. Because now we are so disconnected from our true nature and so entangled with machines that we don't recognize inappropriate tribal reactions to modern problems. And that's a dangerous place to be. The Churn creates these shadows of tribalism—fear, scarcity, group feud, even violence—which trick our left brain into thinking it needs to fight. But I contend that we don't need to fear, when there is abundance all around us. The scarcity is contrived. Feuding is regressive, and violence, while sometimes necessary, is not the answer.

Instead, we need to turn to our right-brain, below-the-waterline selves. We need social connection, we need real reciprocity, we need storytelling, we need to spend time outside in nature, we need to invest in social capital—not just financial capital.

If you want to get shit done, you have to make these things visible. You have to put down your pistol, get your head out of your device, stop blaming others, and step out of your dark closet into the light.

The Ecstasy of Chaos

When our public square is governed by mob dynamics, unrestrained by due process, we don't get justice and inclusion, we get a society that ignores context, proportionality, mercy, and truth.

—Jonathan Haidt

Before moving on and getting MESSSy in the next section of the book—the "practical guide" portion—I want to talk briefly not about the last 10,000 years, 250 years, or 100 years. I want to talk about the last decade or so.

During this time, something new has happened. Something wicked.

The rise of social media over this time has caused us to become even more entangled with our devices and the digital worlds they re-present.

When social media platforms like MySpace and Facebook first emerged in the early 2000s, their ability to bridge divides and connect people was encouraging. However, around 2012, users started to spend more time *performing* and less time *connecting*. The development of "like" and "share" features across these and other platforms accelerated viral dynamics. It was at this time that the "enragement equals engagement" phenomenon began to take hold. Social media companies quickly learned that if people were angry about something, if a post tickled their mob mentality, if it scratched their partisan itch, then people would share it more. This traffic caused more people to stay on their platforms, which enabled the platforms to put more targeted advertising in front of people, which enabled the companies to sell more advertising, which made these businesses inordinately more valuable. Our performative enragement—which we gave away *for free*—made many people embarrassingly rich and put the rest of us deeper into a trance. For them, our anger was the gift that kept on giving.[11]

Perhaps most insidiously, social media remains indispensable for forging some real connections, and it also makes doing business for small operations more feasible. But these weren't the features that made these companies money. It was anger, dishonesty, name-calling, moral superiority, and contempt.

Contempt.

Friends and families—to say nothing of good faith competitors—who stray into contempt won't last long. It's a short step from here to irreconcilable differences. It's a longer step to authoritarianism or civil unrest, but what's certain is that for either to occur a prerequisite is contempt for one's neighbors.[12]

It's gotten so bad, and we've become so tribal, that I'm far more concerned about how we *treat* each other as we discuss our many and varied issues than I am about the issues themselves.

The Churn generally, but social media specifically, amplifies our mutual contempt. We run to our corners, yelling at each other. We physically attack each other. We even shoot at each other. We become divided, and then we become more divided. And for what? So some businessperson you'll never meet can sell more advertising and make more money that they don't need; or so some politician can anger enough people to convince them to vote *against* the other guy rather than *for* themselves so that they can gain or stay in power.

The crazy thing is that this contempt-fueled perpetual motion/money-printing/power-entrenching machine even works. The reason is simple, though, and it has everything to do with our deep, primal nature and the fact that we are unaware of it. You see, when you get these feelings of contempt and moral superiority, you briefly feel good. You get a little hedonical dopamine hit. You feel vindicated. You feel *right*. This is the ecstasy of chaos.

And now, right now, to this chaos we are adding artificial intelligence. Very soon, AI-generated disinformation will flow at an unprecedented rate, further misguiding our perceptions and leveraging our division. How will we know what's real in this environment? If you think agreeing on facts is difficult now, just you wait. Introduce nefarious bad actors like Russia, China, and ISIS, and we'll have an arms race seeking to deploy AI for all the wrong reasons.

At the intersection of all these forces lie the Four Ds mentioned earlier in this book. Our current moment is a force multiplier for distraction, disengagement, disconnection, and distrust. The status quo cannot stand.

Which means it's high time we get MESSSy.

CHAPTER 3

Lead from the Rooftop

What It Takes

How do you break through the trance, get past the Churn, dive below the waterline, give your right brain its due, and emerge from the chaos?

You connect like your life depends on it.

For Green Berets, their lives literally do depend on it. Over the years, I've done a lot of work with young candidates going through Special Forces training. Principally, I've helped them understand that once they deploy, they will be stepping out of the conventional, top-down, blunt-instrument military and into something very different.

As soon as their training is finished and there is a need somewhere in the world, they will be sent to low-trust locations where rapport and influence are essential to winning favorable outcomes. Since the brain is a metaphorical, pattern-matching organ, I have landed on a few well-known avatars for my brand of Rooftop Leadership that don't need much in the way of introductions.

I tell Green Berets they will have to be a mixture of John Wick, Lawrence of Arabia, and the Verizon Guy.

The looks they give me may be similar to the look on your face right now, so I explain, "To be a Rooftop Leader, you'll have to be surgically coercive but only when absolutely necessary; you'll have to rise above the churn of conflict by listening, building trust, and taking account of facts on the ground; but most of all you'll have to connect with people, often radically different than you, like your life depends on it."

The churn of war is different than the Churn I've been discussing so far, mainly because it has the potential to kill you in violent ways. But dealing with our Churn here at home has many of those low-trust, high-stakes qualities and requires these same three archetypes to get past the Four Ds.

Let's take a closer look at each, starting with John Wick.

John Wick

Let's face it. This crazy world sometimes demands coercion, with surgical precision, to protect what we value and to meet our goals. There are many different archetypes to illustrate this reality. I choose John Wick, a fictional ex–hit man pulled back into the dark criminal underworld he once left behind. No matter where he finds himself, John Wick is always in an extremely high level of conflict. But whether he's in a nightclub, a museum, or a hotel lobby, he maintains surgical coercion, only applying his martial skill where needed. That's what Green Berets do as well. Otherwise, the collateral damage to innocent bystanders would be too much. Their coercion is also selective. When they find themselves in tense situations, they don't always turn to their weapons. If they did, they would lose any chance at building trust and being able to wield influence over the long term.

A version of this is true for anyone trying to achieve goals when other people are involved. Unless you're in law enforcement or the military, I'm not suggesting you make use of physical coercion during your daily life, but rather that we keep handy a type of surgical, unbending resolve that is sometimes necessary when faced with conflict. This is a baseline capability all leaders should possess, but one with which we should lead only when necessary.

Lawrence of Arabia

In 1917, at the height of World War I, a young British intelligence officer achieved the impossible. He mobilized Bedouin tribes in what is now Syria and Iraq to set their tribal differences aside and come together to liberate the city of Aqaba from the Ottoman Turks. This was a huge turning point in the war that vastly improved the strategic advantage of Allied forces across the region.

The man was T. E. Lawrence, a.k.a. "Lawrence of Arabia," a former geologist. Although Lawrence was highly decorated for valor, he is most remembered for the interpersonal skills he utilized to build trust in the face of centuries of tribal, status behavior. His work—in word and in deed—is a testament to the power of local engagement and human connection. The "weapons" Lawrence wielded so effectively included storytelling, active listening, and rapport building. So-called soft skills that are anything but.

If our institutional leaders too often malign these skills, bad actors often do not. Some of the world's most dangerous people are masters at leveraging these influence tools to manipulate others to do their terrible bidding. ISIS are excellent storytellers; gang leaders can build rapport; and racist activists build deep bonds of trust within their in-groups to enact their own narrow agendas.

People like this are an unfortunate reality of the Churn and are even worse than simple divisionists, who often act for their own personal gain. If you're going to lead beyond them, it's essential to call bullshit on bad behavior whenever you see it, and even develop ways to isolate and marginalize bad actors so that they become less influential.

But you can't call bullshit if you don't first possess Lawrencian skills that are often derided for no good reason. Lawrence's approach to influence is not Pollyannaish. It requires a well-entrenched moral compass and a penchant for bridging across groups, not dividing them. To do this, instinct is not enough. You must learn it, and you have to practice it, over and over and over again. It's a lifelong pursuit.

Also—these are not soft skills at all—they are hard, in the sense that they are both difficult to master and, if used properly, very difficult to defeat. This is precisely why they are taught at the Special Forces Qualification Course, one of the Army's most hallowed programs.

In today's Churn, where trust is low, the stakes for not developing these skills are too high. If you don't, you risk being lured into the trance state of shadow tribalism, right alongside everyone else.

The Verizon Guy

The Churn is complex. Organizational complexity is a big part of it. There are so many formal and informal groups popping up with multiple subcultures and agendas. For example, if you're a veterans' advocate, there are more than fifty thousand veteran websites to contend with. This can be paralyzing. It's known as the "sea of goodwill."

How do you navigate this kind of complexity when you aren't even sure who is around you? This was the challenge when Afghanistan collapsed and we were trying to figure out how to move our allies through a series of physical and virtual gauntlets, often with kids and older family members in tow. It was like looking at a wicked problem through a soda straw, which is a painful way to navigate the world and find solutions. Coercion pushes people away. Interpersonal skills aren't quite enough.

This is where the Verizon Guy comes in. The final avatar of Rooftop Leadership.

The Verizon Guy runs the seams, phone in hand, building networks of connections. One minute he's in a jungle, asking someone on the other end of the line, "Can you hear me now?" Then he pops out of a manhole cover: "Can you hear me now?" Then he's on a raft in the middle of the ocean: "Can you hear me now?"

Dude is everywhere.

The Verizon Guy is obsessed with connecting across space and time. He sprints across the network, building connections and checking them. He personifies bottom-up leaders who bring disparate but relevant people together around hard problems. He is a catalyst intent on solving wicked problems through collaboration. Once he finishes his job and the connections are made, the Verizon Guy claps his hands and gets out of the way.

But my version of the Verizon Guy goes even further. He doesn't just connect people; he also connects our traditional below-the-waterline status society with our modern above-the-waterline contract society. He has a deep understanding and respect for both the modern world *and* the traditional world. The Verizon Guy is left-brain/right-brain; he keeps one foot above the waterline and one foot below.

One of the greatest challenges the Verizon Guy faces in navigating our complex world is not getting completely sucked into the virtual realm, especially in the rapid evolution of platforms like Signal. I nearly lost my connection to the natural world during an intense period—when I and several others worked together to extract as many Afghan friends and colleagues from their country in the days before it fell to the Taliban. For the most part, we worked remotely, thousands of miles from Kabul and Kandahar, working 24/7 with little sleep, building and leveraging massive networks in the re-presented, virtual domain of a Signal chat room. It was a dark time, not just because the clock was ticking and lives were on the line. It was literally dark: indoors, secluded, staring at screens, the left brain churning, no right-brain awareness of the world around us. We were safe from the Taliban, but we were nonetheless cut off and slowly reinjuring ourselves after years of combat in that country.

This is a massive challenge for any Rooftop Leader: how to remain connected with their humanity as they run the digital seams serving the greater good.

We'll talk about methods for dealing with this later in the book.

Let's Get MESSSy

Over the last decade, I've come up with a framework to help us understand our primal nature, discern the forces that drive us and those around us, and implement it all so that we can rise above the many challenges dragging us down.

I call it MESSS. (Yes, I know, there's an extra S there. Blame my Arkansas public education.) After decades of military and corporate work, I've come to loathe acronyms, but sometimes they're useful. Forgive me.

This refers to the fact that humans are ancient creatures who seek **M**eaning, are primarily **E**motional, are definitively **S**ocial, and are all **S**torytellers who constantly **S**truggle. Let's break it down.

We seek **Meaning**. Humans are meaning-seeking and meaning-assigning creatures. Yet today, the absence of purpose is at an all-time low. We must reclaim purpose in our lives now more than ever before.

Emotions are real. We're not rational beings capable of feeling, we're emotional beings capable of reason. But too often we're cut off from our own emotions, which means we're nearly exclusively cut off from the emotions of others. Regaining access to our emotions and managing our emotional temperature are learned skills, especially now when so many left-hemisphere, trance-state humans are busy raging at the world.

We're **Social**. We don't have fur, fangs, or claws, yet here we are, on top of the food chain. Why is that? Because we are the best in the world at forming teams and groups. Social scientist Matthew Lieberman cites our social skill as our greatest superpower.[13] The irony is that we're losing our social acumen. Relentless emphasis on the individual and the disintegration of social capital coming out of a two-year pandemic has led to unprecedented levels of isolation.

We're **Storytellers**. For tens of thousands of years, storytelling has been the primary tool humans use to make sense of things. Yet today, we find ourselves in a narrative deficit. According to the philosopher Walter Benjamin, "The art of storytelling is coming to an end…It is as if something that seemed inalienable to us, the securest among our possessions, were taken from us: the ability to exchange experiences."[14] The irony is that now, in our mechanistic contract society, people crave stories more than ever. We need to get back to storytelling—if we can't achieve shared perspective on what the world looks like, how can we possibly hope to move forward?

We all **Struggle**. It's universal. The Buddha believed that struggle is brought on by attachment to things—and a thing could be an idea as easily as an object—and that since all things are impermanent, struggle is the result. In any case, struggle is necessary. We all struggle. Period. The more you acknowledge struggle, in yourself and in others, the more relatable you become.

MESSS is a lens we can use to peer both inward and outward at our own human nature. We can use it to look below the surface at the invisible realities that often are at the heart of modern problems like mergers, breakups, and general conflict.

MESSS also provides us with levers to pull for making more intentional decisions, as well as for fostering more authentic human connections.

Ultimately, MESSS is a framework for action. It embodies our biological evolution—our superpowers—which we have inherited over the millennia from the deep roots of our status society. To be clear, I'm not advocating we return to a tribal society. There is a lot to celebrate about living in a world of abundance.

However, we must maintain awareness of our relationship-based, status society roots that often place the group above the individual, and we must simultaneously stay present in our modern world with its freedoms and opportunities that often value the individual above the group. Only then can we reliably connect the past to the present and bring our full humanity to bear on shaping the future. Only then can we avoid navigating the modern Churn by mere instinct. Only then can we escape the trancelike behavior of our competitors and peers and avoid being dragged into unnecessary conflicts. Only then can we create a culture of thriving while others are fighting to survive.

CHAPTER 4

Meaning
or, The Mandate to Make Sense

*Ultimately, man should not ask what the meaning of his
life is, but rather must recognize that it is he who is asked.
In a word, each man is questioned by life; and he can only
answer to life by answering for his own life; to life he can
only respond by being responsible.*

— Viktor E. Frankl, *Man's Search for Meaning*

A Mandate for Meaning

Have you heard of the Alcoholics Anonymous saying, "Clean
your side of the street"? Essentially, it means that you must take
responsibility for your own actions before you can help any-
one else. Put a little differently, it means that you—and only
you—are in a position to help yourself. Other people can be of
assistance, but at the end of the day it's just you.

Similarly, you and only you are responsible for fighting our common enemy, the Churn, and for seeking meaning in your own life. This is true now more than ever, with the waning influence of institutions like media, community clubs, and faith-based organizations.

No one else is coming to save you. This is not a reason to despair—which the Churn wants. It is an opportunity. It is something to celebrate.

Now, I'm not preaching a new kind of religion here. Far from it. But our brain has a mandate to make sense of the world. Much of that meaning comes from serving something bigger than ourselves. So, we need to start there. I want to share the meaning-making tools I use to fight the Churn, to serve the people you lead, and to beat back the darkness for the light.

These tools are Leave Tracks, Surrender to Purpose, Get Clear, Get Back to Where the Wild Things Are, and Get Moving. Let's take them one at a time.

Leave Tracks

"Scott, your dad has cancer," my father's doctor said. "It's stage four non-Hodgkin's lymphoma. The cancer is in his bone marrow. It's very advanced and moving fast. We're going to treat this thing, but I don't know how it'll go."

I was stalled in bumper-to-bumper traffic on the George Washington Parkway outside Washington, DC, when the doctor delivered this news about my dad, Rex. Suddenly, my dull commute turned surreal. Everything else the doctor said turned into the *wah-wah-wah* gibberish of the grown-ups in the *Peanuts* cartoons. I don't remember what else the doctor said except that my dad was tough and was going to fight as hard as he could. I don't remember hanging up the phone. I do remember slamming my fist into the steering wheel over and over as I sat trapped in my barely moving car.

Of course Dad was going to fight. He was always "the Woodsman," an almost mythical figure in my mind, especially when I was young. He grew up in the Great Smoky Mountains just outside Asheville, North Carolina. He'd spent almost forty-two years in the US Forest Service, but he was also a "hot shot" firefighter who flew out west for fire season, hiking into the Rocky Mountains backcountry to fight big wildfires. When I was growing up in a little logging town, the Woodsman would often take my brother, Travis, and me on long walks in the forest for what he called "character building." Along the way, he'd stop and point at fresh animal prints—rabbit, deer, coyote. "Boys, look down there. You see that? I don't care what you decide to do in your life, where you live, or who you marry—just make sure you leave your tracks in this world. You hear me?" We heard him, but we just rolled our eyes and kept traipsing through the woods.

I immediately asked for time off from work and went to Kentucky, where my parents lived. My mom was exhausted, so I took Dad to monthly chemotherapy treatments. One day, I stood in the clinic with my back to the wall, trying not to look at Dad because the smell of disinfectant triggered memories of friends fighting for their lives in Afghan field hospitals.

"You okay, Scotty Doodle?" he asked.

My dad is the only person who can call me "Scotty Doodle." And in that instant, it reminded me of better days. We didn't have much money growing up, but Dad always made sure we were happy. Even in the worst of times, this six-foot-tall, strapping woodsman would pick me up under one arm and my little brother under the other and walk around the house belting out bluegrass songs, us two boys squealing and laughing. To us, he was a giant, as tall as the towering oaks we lived among.

This same man was now diminished, and I barely recognized him. He slumped in his chair, his hair was gone. He had a damn chemo port pumping rat poison into his chest.

I felt like there was a hockey stick in my throat as I choked out, "No, Dad, I'm not okay. I know it's selfish, but I've lost too many friends to war, and I'm not ready to lose you."

He smiled. He waved his hand, motioning for me to sit. I did. "Scotty," he said, "I'm scared too. But think about the wonderful life I've had with your mom. All the good memories of you and your brother and our adventures. And, hey—how about all the wildfire fighters I've mentored over the years. Beautiful relationships. I've left my tracks in this world."

That pummeled me. It shouldn't have, of course, since I'd been hearing that exact phrase my whole life. But it wasn't until that instant, in a cancer ward sitting next to my dying father, that I fully understood it.

I was quite senior in my Army career at that point. I'd been in combat many times, I'd been with warriors when they took their last breaths, and I thought I had leadership all figured out. But as I witnessed his grace and poise in the face of death, my dad showed me I was still learning.

The tracks he referred to were those indelible impressions each of us leave on this earth. We leave tracks whether we mean to or not, but meaningful tracks require intention. It's a choice. It's a series of choices that add up to one's legacy. That's what Dad was saying.

True leaders serve not only the people around them, but also the people who come long after they're gone. These kinds of tracks create clarity. What I finally realized was that *for my whole life* he'd been articulating what I had been practicing but hadn't yet verbalized: Rooftop Leadership. My tracks had helped those desperate Afghan villagers to climb those ladders onto the rooftop in the dark dangers of the night and fight for themselves.

For many months after that, Dad fought. He tapped his innate stubbornness and refused to give in. That old mountain man didn't get the memo that he was terminally ill.

In the end, his cancer went into remission and Dad got one more chance at living. He wasn't finished looking for meaning. He still had tracks to leave.

Children, Cherokee, and Chestnuts

I believe we leave three main types of tracks: tracks for our youth, tracks of capacity, and tracks of relationships. I'm sure there are more, but I see these three a lot. So we can be more intentional in our legacy track-leaving, let's unpack these.

Tracks for our youth. Our kids will leave us sooner than we think. Our inherent responsibility is to do all we can to prepare them for the challenges they'll face. We do this as parents, teachers, and coaches, but anyone can do this work. My dear friend David Martin doesn't have kids but was a big brother to two at-risk teen boys. He taught and mentored and held space for them to grow into amazing young men who are now leading their communities with considerable impact. That's "leaving tracks" in action.

Tracks of capacity. Many leaders today are focused on "success." But what the hell does that mean? It's so transactional and off-putting. No wonder employees are disengaged. When it comes to tracks, I define capacity as the ability of the people you serve to keep moving forward when you are not there. In Special Forces, while helping to build capacity in foreign armies, we call it "working ourselves out of a job." The ultimate tracks are when our efforts continue to serve others long after we're gone. Whether it's at a for-profit or nonprofit organization, the building of capacity has the power to do big things after you leave the job. As my friend Bo Eason says, "Tell people what you're building and then ask them to help. We all want to contribute to a growing capacity that does good work beyond our time."

Tracks of relationships. My dad developed an initiative with the Eastern Band of the Cherokee Indians to create a tree nursery on reservation land, the first of its kind. The entire project was built on the shoulders of a relationship that had been established between his dad, an iconic mountain man named Howard, and a Cherokee elder named Jimbo more than fifty years earlier. The relationship they forged was so strong that it allowed my dad to reconnect with Jimbo, an influential elder, and his son, who sat on the timber committee of the tribal council. If you build strong relationships that are authentic and focused on the other party, you will create levels of reciprocity that span generations.

My dad left another set of tracks too.

Have you heard of the American chestnut tree? Before the Europeans arrived in the New World, the American chestnut was a common hardwood found from Maine to the lower Mississippi and as far west as the eastern plains. It was one of the main hardwoods, along with maple, oak, ash, birch, beech, walnut, and cherry, that defined the Appalachian woodlands. Mature chestnuts could reach a hundred feet or more in height, and their mushroom-cap-like canopy grew to diameters of up to sixty feet. They were essential to the forest ecosystem, providing shelter, food, and shade. And, not least important for an early industrial society, they provided a lot of timber. A single mature American chestnut, whose trunk grew straight up and whose arrow-shot limbs and boughs jutted off at near-perfect right angles, could yield up to fifteen thousand board feet of durable, rot-resistant lumber.

And then, in the early twentieth century, the American chestnut became infected by a fungus from the Asian chestnut tree, to which it had no resistance. Within the span of just a couple decades, as many as four billion trees died. Just like that, more than 99 percent of all of these majestic trees were gone.

Many people have fought for the American chestnut since, Dad included. He reasoned that since we vaccinate humans, why can't we vaccinate trees? Dad was an early adopter of a budding program that leveraged modern genetics to restore a species that was once thought lost forever. Now we are on the cusp of reintroducing this tree to the forest.

My dad was such a fan of the American chestnut that when President George W. Bush invited him to the White House to watch the bill signing for the Healthy Forests Restoration Act of 2003, my dad convinced the president to plant a blight-resistant American chestnut on the White House grounds. It's still there today. In a recent TED Talk my dad gave on the restoration of the American chestnut, he said, "I'll never see this tree in the woods, but my grandkids will."*

That's leaving all three kinds of tracks.

What if we all approached our track-leaving like this? Imagine it's fifteen years after you left this earth and the person who held your hand in your final moments is having dinner with someone you never met. That person asks about you and your legacy. What would your special person say? If you're already working on a legacy, then you'll know. But if you aren't, as is more likely the case, don't fret. Grab a pen and some paper, find a quiet place, and write for seven minutes about the legacy you'd like to leave. A hidden gem will reveal itself, even if it's just barely twinkling.

To fully light up the power of meaning in your life, pursue that gem and leave those tracks with unreasonable audacity.

Surrender to Purpose

Whether you uncover your personal purpose in this way or are lucky enough to be inspired to pursue a genuine organizational purpose, once you can see your purpose you need to run after it. Hard.

---

*If you'd like to see the Woodsman's storytelling in action, you can check out my dad, Rex's TED Talk he did on the American chestnut, right after recovering from cancer, here: https://youtu.be/zwvlY8Hll3c.

When we were working to save our Afghan partners before the fall of Kabul, running the digital seams in our nonstop, 24/7 Signal chat room, we did just that. When it was all said and done, there were tens of thousands of texts and voice messages. When I went back through the archives, I found zero entries about Donald Trump and only one about Joe Biden.

How could this be? With our country so divided, and with so much blame to pass around for the state of the withdrawal, and with so many different kinds of people in the Signal thread, it seemed impossible. Each of us had reasons to be pissed at both leaders. So why no rants or tirades?

Purpose.

Every member of our operation was laser-focused on our collective purpose: to honor a promise to our allies to ferry them to safety. There wasn't time for anything else. Everything else flowed from there.

That's the power of purpose, and of surrendering to it.

Without purpose, we perish. At minimum, we point fingers and yell. We lose, the Churn wins.

Get Clear

On the eve of our twenty-eighth wedding anniversary, my wife, Monty, and I went to Jamaica for vacation. I was in bad shape. I was exhausted from a grueling road schedule of speeches and performances (I'd been acting in the lead role of a play I'd written that had been touring the country—more on that later). The Israel-Hamas war had sucked me deeper into the world of mobile devices. I was back on Signal nonstop, which I hate passionately. My available time was measured in minutes, not hours—and certainly not the days required to properly be on vacation. You send an email, I respond in minutes. You comment on my LinkedIn post, I respond in seconds. I was angry, moody, and I could feel my blood pressure going through the roof.

The Churn—which I also have to fight off constantly—had me by the balls.

When Monty and I arrived at our little villa on the Caribbean, I felt slightly better. This would be our fourteenth trip here. The air was salty and inviting. But work hung over me. I was starting this book and continuing a few other projects. I wasn't ready to relax.

That first night I woke up around 1:00 a.m. to go to the bathroom because, well, I'm fifty-five and that's my life. As I walked back to bed, my phone buzzed and glowed, beckoning me in the darkness. I picked it up. "Shit," I said louder than intended.

"What's the matter, baby?" Monty asked groggily.

"The Israel-Palestine situation is getting worse."

"Okay, so put your phone down," Monty said. "There's nothing you can do about it. You're going to stroke out if you keep responding to every situation this way."

That floored me, but she was right. I had been sucked into every crisis since the Afghanistan collapse and I was a wreck.

I switched my phone off and went to bed. Sleep did not return easily, but eventually I drifted off.

The next morning, I looked at my phone with disgust. I was tempted to learn more about the Middle East crisis, but I was numb. The October 7 massacre made me sick, but I dimly realized that my phone also made me sick. I reached for it reflexively, hesitated, and spun away. As I left the bedroom, I felt my anxiety grow. *Just a few hours*, I thought. *I can go a few hours without it, right?*

I could, and I did, but boy was it difficult. It felt a little like when I'd quit alcohol so many years back. But maybe because I'd done that successfully, I fought the urge.

A few hours later, my toes started to uncurl. I let out some big exhales. I felt increasingly grounded. Sitting on the beach, the waves seemed louder. The air saltier. The sky bluer.

As the sun set, Monty observed, "You haven't checked your phone all day. You okay?"

"I'm more than okay," I said. "I'm going to leave it off tonight too."

Which I did. I also left it off the next day.

And the next.

And the next.

All told, I ended up doing a seven-day digital detox. It was game-changing. The clarity and creativity I experienced was freeing. The reclamation of my agency was incredible. As the days passed—and as Monty also turned off her phone—we talked more than we otherwise would have. We calculated that I hadn't turned my phone off for that long in at least a decade.

As I said, I started this book on that trip. It was in Jamaica that I first made use of the term "the Churn." As the days passed, I came to appreciate our common enemy more and more. It helped that I named it. And I came to realize that the quickest, most direct way to take a break from the Churn is to turn off your phone.

It's unlikely we'll get big shit done without these devices, but we must beware of the potential they have for paralyzing us. Dr. Yousef suggests a better "digital hygiene." A less extreme but nearly as effective way to deal with the impingements of our digital devices is to shut off all notifications on your mobile device. Try it. Cut these highly addictive features out of your day and see what happens. Stop the social media, news, shopping, and game notifications and witness how much time you can reclaim of your life from your phone. If you miss one or two of these, add them back, but be intentional about it.

What happens to you when you turn off your phone will be different than what happened to me. It is like opening a sluicegate on a diverted stream. Whatever was running back there before will, in short order, come running over. Maybe you read more, or exercise more, or knit more, or draw more, or cook more, or call friends more, or walk more, or cuddle with the dog more, or cuddle with your partner more. Or all of it.

Whatever you end up doing will come because of having more clarity. If the Churn has an opposite, it is clarity. Getting even a small dose of this will feed your right brain's innate need to connect to the natural world and deprive your left brain of its ability to return you to the part of the Churn defined by the entangled mess of our re-presented virtual realms. It will free you from all the bullshit tasks you think you're supposed to do to feed the status performance machine of social media, being informed, and staying entertained (and being shown advertising the whole way through).

Seriously, ask yourself, when was the last time you shut down your devices? Or went fully offline for eight hours? What runs through your mind when I say that? Does your heart start racing? Do you get antsy?

Good. Don't run from that anxiety. Run toward it.

Don't worry about how you'll run your business. Don't worry about your clients. Your kids will be fine. Your emails will still be there when you return. None of it is going anywhere.

If you have the capacity and the inclination, do it for a number of days, not just a number of hours. If you're anything like me and it's been years—if you are, quite literally, totally entangled with the digital world—then gaining clarity will take at least a couple days. I didn't even start to feel like I was out of my head and back in my body until I was forty-eight hours into it.

It's crazy town, I know, but I'm suggesting a digital detox of forty-eight to seventy-two hours at least once every quarter. (Currently I do this once a quarter as well as one twenty-four-hour digital detox once per month.) I am also challenging you to set a window in the mornings for zero screen time, and all screens off at least one hour before you rack out for the night.

I don't think that a single detox will do it. Integration into your daily rhythm and your working calendar is a must. Breaking the entanglement on a recurring basis, in a way that works for you, is essential to opening you up to the meaning you're seeking. It will also give you the mental, physical, and spiritual energy to surrender to your purpose, once you figure out what that is.

Time is not on our side here. Our left-hemisphere delusion and obsession with imitation of the machine has us in a tough spot. With the rate of entanglement we're sinking into, and with new levels of AI on the horizon, if we don't integrate these digital detox sessions into our bones, we might reach a point of no return. More than a few social scientists and digital engineers have nervously muttered about species extinction. At that point, reclaiming this time will no longer be an option.

Clean your side of the street. In all likelihood, nobody, and I mean nobody, is going to make you get clear. That's your personal responsibility. As the above-the-waterline world demands more of our bandwidth and spiritual energy, we must build a lifelong regimen for reclaiming our clarity. People follow clarity. Besides, without clarity, we aren't fully human.

Get Back to Where the Wild Things Are

We know that the modern world drives our left brain to be distracted, disengaged, and disconnected, and that it actively foments distrust. It hits all of the Four Ds.

One way to deal with these is to undertake a regimen of digital detoxes. Another way—especially when it comes to being disconnected—is to get outside. When we allow the Churn to dominate us, we lose our connection to the natural world. When we lose our connection to the natural world, we lose the connection to others. Isolation follows.

As with digital detoxing, getting outside will reclaim some time from our harried lives, but it does so much more. It grounds us in our bodies, and reaffirms what is real, the wild things, both inside and out.

My dad always said, "If you want to get back to human nature, get back to nature." I couldn't agree more.

For the record, I'm not talking about that once-a-year trip to a fishing village that doesn't have internet, causing you to white-knuckle it for forty-eight hours. I'm talking about an ongoing, intentional reconnection with the natural world and the grounding experience that comes with it.

Sit around a fire and tell a story. Go camping. Meditate by the water. Go for a hike. If you hate hiking and you have no intention of ever sleeping in a tent, don't worry. Sit on a beach. Buy a canoe and use it. Lie on your roof and count stars. Buy a telescope and set it on a hill. Take an outdoor yoga class. Sit still and draw the flowers in your yard. Pull weeds in your garden. Make a birdhouse and hang it. Dig a hole. Watch some birds. Pick berries. Sit by a stream. Get a metal detector and take it out to the cornfield. Use the park. Walk every block in your neighborhood. Adopt a dog and take it out for walks. Climb a rock wall. Go fishing, go hunting. Grow beans and bring them inside for canning. Lace up your sneakers and go for a run. Feed the hummingbirds and watch them eat. Ride a horse. You get the idea. Treat these endeavors with care. They are sacred. The time they take and the spaces they inhabit are also sacred. What I mean is that there is a spiritual component to getting outside. The natural world has the power to shatter our fear-based, trance state and restore our sense of meaning and our connections, not just between ourselves and our environment, but between one another. We must give these actions the intentional respect they deserve.

Our mechanistic world and our left brain's quest for control will pull at you and try to talk you out of these pursuits. They will try like hell to tug you back. That's the Churn. It knows that the effort you make to reconnect to the natural world is an ongoing series of actions that are, once appreciated, self-perpetuating. They weaken the Churn's sway over you. They nurture the right brain's desire to see itself in context, in community, under trees, on the grass, on a road or path of your own choosing, looking up in wonder. The Churn knows that as soon as you find an outdoor pursuit you enjoy, you will want to do it again and again, no matter what it is. It would prefer you not find this treasure you hid from yourself and forgot all about.

When I facilitate coaching sessions with strategic leaders, we get off grid and spend most of our working time around a fire pit. These kinds of reclamation projects will pay immediate dividends in your other pursuits. They will help contextualize your efforts to get shit done. They will make you a better Rooftop Leader. These projects are worth it. They mean more space in your mind, body, and spirit, less anxiety, and more capacity to leave tracks of legacy.

Get Moving

It took me a while to realize it after I left the Army, but I'm a creative dude. My thirst for relevance is directly proportional to my desire to create. For me, it's simple. My creative search for meaning has kept me out of the darkness that nearly caused me to take my own life.

I once asked a former Delta Force operator how he manages to run so hard in his civilian life and he replied, "Sir, I'm like a great white shark. If I stop moving, I'll die." That made immediate sense. The meaning I've found never came to me while I passively sat frozen waiting for answers.

It came to me through movement.

The idea for writing the play I mentioned earlier came to

me when I was out on a run. I decided to write a book about veterans transitioning into civilian life while on a long walk following the attempted suicide of one of my Army buddies. Facing mounting debt, I started imagining building a commercial real estate portfolio as I washed my hair in the hot shower.

According to the psychiatrist and educator Ivan Tyrrell, "Movement and meaning are inextricably linked." In fact, he says, "A truly spiritual person is not a hermit sitting on a mountain contemplating his navel, but someone involved in the world, working, serving others and opposing tyranny of all kinds."[15]

The prescription here is simple: When you are feeling stuck, move. The more stuck you are, the darker your grief or anxiety, the more you need to move. The left hemisphere will resist and try to convince you to just stew on it or look for a logical solution.

That's bullshit.

Move. Lift weights. Hit the heavy bag. Go for a walk. Even meditation involves dynamic movement of the diaphragm.

When we move, even if we don't know the answer to the problem—hell, especially if we don't know the answer to the problem—the muse will often hand over the gift of clarity as we wipe the pouring sweat from our brow or feel the Jell-O in our legs from a long run.

If your kid, coworker, or former squad mate from the Marine Corps is hurting or stuck, encourage them to move. Move with them.

Because movement and meaning are inextricably linked.

CHAPTER 5

Emotion
or, How to Navigate a Shovel Fight

When the emotional brain takes over, it locks our atten-
tion on what has aroused us, to the increasing exclusion
of other information from the environment. This focus
means we are seeing reality from only one particular per-
spective because in this type of trance the higher cortex is
less engaged in reality checking. You can see this clearly
when someone gets angry, and you cannot reason with
them. In anger, a person is totally focused on their own
point of view and will appear stupid.

—Ivan Tyrrell, *The Human Givens*

Last Out

"Scott, you should write a play about the war." This came from
my friend and mentor Bo Eason one day in 2015.

It was so out of the blue that I wasn't sure I'd heard him right. "What's that?"

"Put your story up on the stage," he implored. "It's a helluva way to hit people right in the chest. That's what I did with my one-person play about becoming an NFL player, and it gave me a platform I could stand on. It got all the way to Off-Broadway. You'll probably heal a lot of people along the way." He paused, then added, "You might even heal yourself."

Naturally, the idea scared the shit out of me. So I protested. "I'm not a playwright. I don't know anything about acting. I'm fifty-one years old, dude."

"So what?" he said each time. Then he added, "You better get started. You're not getting any younger." We shared a laugh; he cleared his throat. "Listen, man. You're going to do this, and when you do, you're going to have to get real. There is so much emotional charge in this. You've learned how to armor up and push emotions down for twenty years. Now it's the opposite. If you're going to help people recover, you'll need access to those emotions. You'll have to share stories you don't want people to hear. Hell, you'll have to put down stuff *you* don't want to hear."

After we hung up, I thought, *A play? A play about what?*

Not too long afterward, while I was out on a run, it came to me: a play about my experience as a soldier. One of the oldest kinds of plays around.

I wrote furiously for three years. I found writing coaches like Michael Hauge, Jason Cannon, and Chris Crowe. As I wrote, I decided I would play the lead. Bo put me in touch with extremely talented acting coaches like Larry Moss and Karl Bury, who took me under their wings. I wanted this story to be told by those who'd lived it, so I cobbled together a cast of combat veterans and military family members. In early 2018, we began rehearsals in our director's spare bedroom.

The play became *Last Out: Elegy of a Green Beret*. It tells the story of the fictional Army sergeant Danny Patton, mortally wounded in action by an IED in Kandahar Province. It's set in purgatory, where Danny is visited by an old friend who died at the Pentagon on 9/11. The friend's job: Work with other fallen warriors to make sure Danny lets go of his pain so that he can ascend to Valhalla (a.k.a. warrior heaven) and avoid eternal damnation. The story is told primarily in flashbacks; all are based on real events from my life and the lives of other special operators I've known. The flashbacks occur all over, from dusty Afghan villages to emotionally charged stateside living rooms, from honky-tonk Army bars to Danny's homemade "Wall of Honor" shrine. In the end, the play is about much more than war. It's unapologetic and raw, constantly leveraging emotional battle scars to pierce through the Churn. Think *It's a Wonderful Life* but with body armor.

We set Veterans Day 2018 for our premiere. No one had ever heard of us. Why would they? When no theaters would rent us space, my wife and I invested our own money in a hotel ballroom with 362 seats. We didn't have lights or sound, so we rented that too. We walked the streets of Tampa handing out fliers. We pushed the word out on Facebook. My wife and I invested every spare penny we had.

The pressure of such an off-the-wall undertaking took a heavy toll on both of us. Resistance kicked in hard. "Why do you want to do this so badly?" Monty yelled at a particularly stressful time, mere hours before the premiere. "Why are you bringing all this shit up after we've moved on?"

I looked at the window and thought of all the buddies I'd lost. Of all the Danny Pattons I hadn't yet let go of myself.

"Because I'll die if I don't," I whispered.

She looked at me for a long time. Tears streaked her cheeks. Then she smiled and took both of my hands. Finally, she said, "Well, I guess we have a play to put on, then."

The *big shit* was officially on.

I peeked out from the wings at our audience. Every one of those 362 seats was filled. It was a mix of "exhausted majority" Americans who don't normally sit in the same zip code, much less the same room. There were Republicans and Democrats. Marines. Air Force. Navy. Army. Law enforcement. Vietnam-era veterans. Post-9/11 veterans. Green Beret veterans. Politicians. Liberal media. Local business owners. Gold Star families.* Civilians from the arts and theater worlds who had never been around military folks. There were also quite

---

*A family who lost a family member (husband or wife, son or daughter, mom or dad, brother or sister, niece or nephew) in combat.

a few wounded warriors. Some of my old Green Beret team-mates, my parents, my brother, my wife, and our three boys were there. It was a good turnout. Best I could have hoped for.

I was scared out of my mind. Minutes before curtain, I dry-heaved my guts out as the audience waited for the lights to go down.

The play opened with a heart-pounding combat scene, an emotional breaching tool, grabbing the audience by the throat. What followed was a two-hour, white-knuckle roller coaster. When it was over, all four of us cast members stood sweating in our spots, hearts pounding, hands shaking. A spotlight pinned me to the stage. My knees were weak. The ballroom was utterly silent. No one in the audience moved. I closed my eyes and cringed. *They hated it*, I thought.

Hell with it. We did our best.

Then, a roar.

The crowd erupted into a standing ovation that lasted for over five minutes. We bowed, left the stage, then returned for a curtain call. After that, we sat and held a Q-and-A session.

One year after that first performance, the play had grown into a seventeen-person production company of veterans and military family members. We put twenty-eight thousand miles on a U-Haul van that toured sixteen cities across America, from New York City to Washington, DC, to Vermillion, South Dakota, to Brandon, Mississippi, to Santa Barbara, California. Every show revealed a new miracle of storytelling as we bridged the civilian-military gaps of isolation and moral injury that were—and remain—so prevalent across our country.*

And then—COVID hit.

Everything stopped. It wiped out the entire tour. We were forced to shelve the play right when it was gaining momentum. No one was going to sit in a stuffy theater for two hours with a highly contagious pandemic raging, and even if they wanted to, no venues would take the risk. After a few months, I realized that the worst part was that our veterans were racked with the impacts of COVID and the isolation that went with it. It took a toll on me too. I wanted to get back on the stage, share my story, and meet people wherever they were.

Sometime in 2021, I grew tired of my isolation and the isolation of our veterans. Monty and I raised a quarter million dollars through our nonprofit, and we shot a film of *Last Out* using mostly veteran camera crews. We edited it ourselves and put it on Amazon Prime.

Emotion was at the heart of the entire project. Bo had been right. I was sharing stuff I thought I'd never share. I was even revealing things to myself that I'd buried or forgotten. And these revelations rippled out among the people who saw the play, who made meaning out of their own lived experience, who shared their own emotional stories with me, who revealed their own forgotten or suppressed memories. We were paying tribute to a war

---

*If you want to learn more about *Last Out* you can visit lastoutplay.com.

we'd fought. To the men and women who'd died. To our own tortured existences. To the families who stood with us. And to the ones who no longer could. To the dead. To the living.

The stage taught me lessons. Surprising lessons.

I learned about managing emotional temperature as I navigated the Churn. I learned about anger, that most left-brain of all emotions. I learned how to negotiate better. I learned how to navigate change. I learned that I was still quite emotional, but that I could harness my intense feelings for good. I learned to accept those feelings.

I learned that people hurt themselves—even kill themselves—because they don't know what to do with their emotions. I learned it doesn't have to be that way.

I learned to recover.

Let's take a closer look at each.

Emotional Temperature

Our left-brain, above-the-waterline, transactional contract society has a message for us. A loud message. It's a message I heard day after day as a combat soldier. It's: "Push your emotions down and leave them there."

But that's not how we're wired.

If we were among a group of people walking along ten thousand years ago and were jumped by a saber-toothed tiger, we would immediately go into a state of fight, flight, or freeze. This is when our sympathetic nervous system takes over and causes us to react. (Interestingly, the Greek root of "sympathetic" combines *syn*, which means "together with," and *pathos*, which means "feeling" or "suffering." A "sympathetic reaction" in this context refers not only to the sympathetic nervous system taking over but also to how all of us who are attacked by the tiger are drawn closer together through suffering.)

When our sympathetic nervous system hijacks our body, it places our mind in a trance state of extreme focus, with its sole mission being survival.

Let's say we fight back, and the tiger runs off without getting a meal. Some of us die, others are wounded. We limp back to our cave. We bury the dead and treat those who have been injured. We build fires. We cook. We grieve. We eat. We tell stories. We honor. We remember. We share lessons learned for future battles.

On the back end of the attack, it is necessary that we access our emotions. We need to metabolize the trauma of the tiger attack collectively. We do this through human connection. This is where our parasympathetic nervous system takes control. We become calm and introspective. We rest. We digest.

The sympathetic nervous system works to address threats; the parasympathetic works to metabolize the trauma of surviving those threats. They work together to make us who we are and enable us to connect with one another in the face (and aftermath) of struggle. (It's not unlike the working relationship between the left and right hemispheres of our brain.)

Fast-forward to the present day. We're not in caves anymore and the saber-toothed tiger is extinct. We live in a modern contract society of our own creation, but these ingrained human systems are still in effect. Escaping their dictates would be as difficult—and impossible—as removing our own skin for the night and hanging it on a hook until morning. We're still primal.

But that doesn't mean our modern contract society is all that amenable to this tribal setup. Nor should we ignore the signs when this primal, trance state shows up in our modern life.

Our sympathetic nervous system is great for dealing with a tiger attack, but not so great at dealing with a 401(k) as it loses half its value in two months. Fight, flight, or freeze ain't gonna help you with your investment portfolio. But the ancient part of our brain doesn't care. It still kicks us into that elevated emotional state, for the simple reason that it doesn't know the difference between an aggressive tiger and a tanking 401(k).

This is a major problem for our ancient brain as it tries to navigate our mechanistic, consumer-driven world pummeling us with an endless stream of digital saber-toothed tigers.

Unfortunately, the Churn has created a sustained, elevated state of fear that our nervous system is simply not accustomed to dealing with. High levels of stress are the result. And when we're stressed in this way, we don't treat each other as well. We find it harder and harder to be "together with" our common "suffering." We have a hell of a time being sympathetic.

We're not wired to deal with saber-toothed tiger attacks every second of every day. That's not how the natural world works. Our emotional temperature is staying in the elevated red zone way too much, and we end up exploding into trance-state survival mode far too often. This takes away our ability to empathize, it takes away our autonomy, and it makes it easier for divisionists to exploit our trance state for their own selfish ends.

Emotions are necessary for engagement. But our current primal emotional experience is usually inappropriate for the modern problems we're facing. Our constant challenge is to manage, but not suppress, this emotional temperature. Emotions are contagious in the Churn. Making a human connection and gaining initial rapport is essential before commencing with your agenda. Asking thoughtful, open-ended questions that allow the other party to respond in narrative. Striving to see the pictures in their head that drive their goals and illuminate their pain. Engaging with an intention of pure curiosity and discovery. Preparing your body through breathwork for being relatable and relevant before the next tense presentation to your boss begins. These simple moves exponentially reduce the emotional temperature in the room.

Just like flying on an airplane, you put your own oxygen mask on first. You must bring your own emotional temperature down so that you can then bring it down for others. You must reach deep so that you can lead people—people who are often

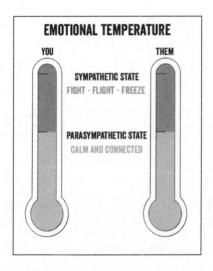

afraid and angry—into a parasympathetic state of calm and connection. Only then can we talk about the modern iterations of our many tiger attacks. Only then can we hear each other. Only then can we lead through the Churn and get shit done.

How to Navigate a Shovel Fight

"Medic!" Carl called on his radio. "We need ambulances at gate two. Now!" The Special Forces team sergeant motioned for the Afghan guards to carefully approach three filthy Toyota pickup trucks. Wounded men screamed from the vehicle beds as others, dressed in traditional Afghan garb, lowered tailgates. "Johnny," Carl said to his interpreter. "Tell them to put their weapons on the ground and let the guards search them." *Security first*, he thought. *Then we'll get to the bottom of this fiasco.*

Three rifles were placed on the ground and the guards patted down each man, even the wounded, who continued to moan and cry out. They were crumpled and bleeding, each on their own stretcher. Next to them was a collection of bloody shovels.

The ambulances soon arrived, and they had to get these men to them ASAP. The senior medic grabbed one end of a stretcher and started to pull. "Holy..." he whispered. The man's face was completely caved in on one side. It was one of the worst wounds the medic had seen. What happened here?

As soon as the injured men were in the ambulances, the medics applied tourniquets and gave the wounded IVs, and a short while later the ambulances took off for the nearby camp clinic, followed by a cloud of dust. Hopefully the men would make it.

Carl turned back to the five uninjured men who'd brought them their wounded. They were twenty feet away, being watched over by his Afghan guards. He grabbed Johnny and they walked over to them. *Just another day in Afghanistan*, Carl thought.

Two of the men squatted together, and the other three stood separately, casually smoking. Everyone watched Carl with interest, and a total absence of fear.

"Let's get to the bottom of this," Carl said to Johnny.

Johnny began speaking to the men. The squatters responded first, but the smokers chimed in, and the discussion got heated. The squatters stood and started pointing at the trucks.

"They keep talking about the shovels," Johnny explained to Carl.

The argument continued for a minute or more before the Afghan guards broke it up and quieted everyone down. Johnny talked to them for a while longer, and then turned to Carl.

"The wounded men come from two clans who live in a nearby valley," Johnny explained. "Apparently, one clan doesn't have enough water to farm. That's what started it."

"Shit," Carl said.

Johnny continued. "This morning, Jan Mohammed, that's the one with the caved-in head, decided to redirect a branch of the river. He went with three of his brothers to dig a trench on the other clan's land. Sabir, the patriarch of the other tribe, noticed them trespassing and grabbed his sons and brothers to confront them. Then, the *tarburwali* started."

"*Tarbuwali*?" Carl asked, wiping sweat from his forehead.

"A blood feud between cousins," explained Johnny.

"Nice."

"Yep. Anyway, after that, words were exchanged, and then Sabir's younger brother attacked Jan Mohammed with his shovel."

"Damn!" Carl exclaimed.

Johnny ignored him. "Then everyone started fighting with

their shovels. After the dust settled, these guys—who weren't involved—brought them here."

Carl and the Afghan guards stayed with the five men until they heard back from the medic. Their wounds were serious, but most of them would make it. Except for Jan Mohammed, the man with the caved-in face. He'd died on the way to the hospital.

Carl sighed at this news. He wiped the sweat from his brow again. The sun was blistering. It was incredibly hot. And tomorrow was supposed to be hotter still.

A bad forecast for an active blood feud between cousins.

He had to get the leaders of these two tribes in the same room to talk this out.

They would have to *negotiate*.

One definition for a negotiation is two or more parties coming together to meet their goals. If you buy that definition, and I do, then it feels like we're negotiating all the time.[16]

One of the most important skills we can bring to any negotiation is managing emotional temperature. When emotions are high—when there is anger or fear—it's difficult for either party to focus on anything beyond survival. The reaction is primal—we can't help it. This level of emotional temperature puts everyone into a trance state that is a less bloody, but just as ineffective, version of a shovel fight.

Two days later, Carl and his team went to the village intent on resolving the dispute. He was calm and collected. And this led to the others being calm and collected. As the emotional temperature settled, they were ready to listen, and they did. They got to the heart of the issues and resolved the feud. Thankfully, the shovel fight did not make it to the negotiating table (or, more accurately, to the rug on the floor).

The same is true for you. You may not be dealing with life-or-death shovel fights over water, but our Churn-induced conflicts can cause us to be just as primal. Reorganizations in your nonprofit. Interteam suspicions within a small business. Divorce arbitration. Political disagreements at a town hall. A sullen teenager intent on staying home from school. Whatever the challenge, emotions are always simmering beneath every negotiation and a feud is just around the corner. If you want to meet your goals, you must keep your cool, and manage emotional temperature always.

Managing the Change Freakout

Let's pivot to business for a moment and consider a hypothetical company about to make a huge organizational change—a merger. Let's pretend you're the one in charge.

Most people hate change. They crave order. On paper, the deal makes total financial sense, but the merger you're about to announce is going to scare the shit out of your people. You know it, they know it. "Is my job secure?" "Will I have enough to feed my family?" "Will my title change when we join this new company?"

Change associated with our livelihood brings out a primal, fear-based response. How do you handle these fears about resource scarcity and status within the group? Are you planning on logically presenting your plan using a thirty-five-slide PowerPoint deck? Do you think that will work?

Well, it may show the logical, financial merits of the merger, but it sure as shit isn't going to help your employees manage their emotions so they can make sense of an epic change in their life when their arena is already uncertain.

Logic doesn't move people. Emotions do.

The next time you have to make a change like this, try something different. Gather all the affected employees and ask them, "What do we all stand for? What are we about? What is the company fighting for?"

Allow them to answer. Write these down on a whiteboard where everyone can see them.

Then point at their answers and synthesize them. "Is this right? Is this who we are? Is this what we stand for?"

They'll likely say, "Yep, that's it."

Then respond, "Okay. This merger is going to go through. I can't promise how everything is going to go, but I give you my word I'll do my best to fight for what's on this board. Would it be okay if I share with you how we must change to do that?" This is a pathway to address emotional temperature and get your folks ready to listen so that they feel like they have a shared future in the journey.*

This approach works well anytime your collective is facing deep change, even your family. It takes a little work, but successfully navigating change starts with managing the emotional temperature in the room.

Emotional Acceptance, Emotional Recovery

I lost seven friends on my first deployment to Afghanistan, and more than that came home wounded. I accompanied the bodies of two of the men who'd been killed in action to their funerals back in the States and spent a lot of time with their families. It definitely took a toll on me.

When I was getting medically tested to go back to war a second time, my lab results were off the charts. High blood pressure. Hypertension. The residual impacts of stress from my last deployment had taken their toll on me. It was obvious that I was going to have to make some major adjustments to how I dealt with emotional stress if I was going to be able to function.

Leadership—whether you're an Army captain leading

---

*This approach was suggested to me by Dr. Kendall Haven, author of *Story Proof* and *Story Smart*, when he was a guest on my podcast. His comment was around change management, and I've since modified it to make it even more accessible to leaders in a broader range of change events.

Green Berets, a high school soccer coach, or a small business owner—is defined as the management of energy.[17] Leaders must be adept at moderating emotional temperature, allowing space for anger to dissipate, and for accepting emotional responses in general. Leaders don't just have to do this for themselves, but also for anyone they are leading. Expending energy in the service of others is mentally, physically, and spiritually exhausting work.

Those back-to-back deployments taught me an essential fact and skill about leadership in the service of others: Recovery is necessary for leadership.

If you're going to get big shit done, there are two types of recovery I recommend.

The first is "micro recovery." These are episodic resets that you can do at any time during your day. Five belly breaths after sitting with an associate who just lost her mom. Ten burpees and a walk around the block after letting someone go from your team. A lip trill making motorboat sounds as you sit in bumper-to-bumper traffic when you're late for an important meeting. The goal of these is simple rituals, dynamic physical movements, or small sensations to get you out of your head and regulate your emotional temperature throughout the course of the day.

The second is "macro recovery." These target and even zero out the deep-seated, cumulative emotional baggage you carry day-to-day. These are rituals that are planned and require more time. Date night. A "staycation" after giving a big keynote. Don't forget that digital detox. A trip to the mountains after a long project has finally been completed. These need to be scheduled on your calendar. Protected vigorously. If not, they are usually the first thing we sacrifice when life throws a surprise our way. This bleeds us dry and leaves us empty. We reach the "finish line" a shell of our former selves.

Leaders building big things don't just perform recovery for themselves. They teach the people they're leading about these tools, and they encourage them to try them as well.

The alternative to not accepting your emotional stresses or actively seeking ways to recover from them is the act of burying emotions. We unconsciously do this all the time, even those of us who are practiced at recovery, just so we can stay in the game or complete some tasks. A lot of this is ego. Doing this never pays dividends, and it always exacts a price. I've seen emotional repression take out some of the most elite warriors on the face of the earth. Delta Force. SEALs. It almost took me out in my closet that day back in 2015.

As I hinted a few lines up, acceptance and recovery take practice. Our modern Churn isn't helping, nor does it want to help. Pushing down emotions in the context of our modern existence also creates a kind of machine-imitation feedback loop: The more we push down our emotions, the more mechanistic we become, causing us to push down our emotions even more. Rinse and repeat. This process is killing our kids, our veterans, our first responders. It's killing you and me. Over the last five years, I've lost nine friends to suicide. These were high-performing individuals who pushed their hurt and anger down—deeper and deeper and deeper—until they couldn't reach them anymore or even name them to tell you what it was they were feeling. The only way they could relieve the agonizing pressure was through self-harm.

There is a prevailing ethos in our modern world that labels unfortunate developments as "just business" or some variation thereof. It's never just business. That is repression in so many words. It's utter bullshit. No matter what we say or try to convince ourselves of, we navigate the world using emotion. But these days, we are so disconnected from our nature and so inundated with fear that we are in a permanent state of semiconsciousness, unaware of how our primal emotions are getting the best of us. This is why we engage in our own shovel fights. We harbor inexplicable grudges, or abandon old friendships over politics, or refuse to listen to our kids when they're pleading their case about what we dismiss as some typical teenage transgression.

Bottom line: No matter how tough you are, give emotions their due. Accept them. Share them in an authentic way. It makes you relatable. But then, recover from their effects. And then, be intentional in helping others manage their emotional temperature. Otherwise, like lava from a simmering volcano, our emotions will erupt into inappropriate responses of shadow tribalism to modern problems. Take the advice of my friend Bo, who encouraged me to put my feelings up on the stage.

You'll heal some people along the way. Hell, you might even heal yourself.

CHAPTER 6

SOCIAL

or, Connect Like Your Life Depends on It

The single most common finding from a half-century's research on the correlates of life satisfaction, not only in the US but around the world, is that happiness is best predicated by the breadth and depth of one's social connections.

—Robert Putnam

Lawrence of Afghanistan

In April 2003, Green Beret Jim Gant led a mission to form a strategic alliance with the Mohmand tribe in eastern Afghanistan. This was a non-Taliban, warlike tribe that inhabited the Kunar River valley. They'd been at odds with the US coalition since the war's inception, and they were headed by an eighty-two-year-old mujahideen named Noor Afzal.

Jim knew that if he was going to be successful, he would need to win over Noor Afzal. So he asked for a meeting. It was risky, even by Green Beret standards. Jim and his small Special Forces team were going to drive deep into mountainous terrain and allow themselves to be surrounded one hundred to one. So you can imagine how palpable the tension was when Jim showed up, took off his body armor, and left his weapon by the door before sitting with Noor Afzal.

The first thing Jim did was to look Noor Afzal in the eye and atone for the last several years of conflict between his tribe and the coalition forces.

This brought the emotional temperature down dramatically.

Then Jim flipped his laptop open and showed raw video footage of the 9/11 attacks on the World Trade Center. Jim sat there, silent, as Noor Afzal watched victim after victim plunge to their deaths to escape the oppressive heat of those doomed buildings on that September day.

When the video ended, Noor Afzal turned to Jim and said, "In all the years that you Americans have been here, no one has ever shown me that. I understand why you're here now."

From there, the real talks began. They lingered, continuing deep into the night. The two men spoke just as much about their pasts as they did about the war. At some point, Jim talked about growing up poor in the badlands of Las Cruces, New Mexico, and of his love for the Native American tribes of the old days. In particular, Jim talked about the legendary Lakota

Sioux chief Sitting Bull, who'd led a successful guerrilla campaign against US forces in the late nineteenth century.

Jim paused and said, "The way you fought the Soviets as mujahideen—you remind me of Sitting Bull." The elders chuckled and the old man smiled beneath his white beard. From that day forward, Noor Afzal had a new name. Until the day he died, and even after adopting Jim as his own son, he was Sitting Bull. Even his family called him this.

When the meeting ended, the stage had been set. The strategic relationship that formed between Jim and Sitting Bull was so powerful that Osama bin Laden would write to his intelligence chief that it was one of the greatest threats to the Taliban in eastern Afghanistan.

That is the power of making social connections. Not a soft skill at all. The complete opposite. The foundation of success.

Connect Like Your Life Depends on It

Relationships are strategic assets. Social capital is at the heart of how people, teammates, employees, and clients take action. Social capital is comprised of the tangible and intangible linkages between you and other people. Rapport. Loyalty. Reciprocity. You get the idea.

If your goal is to inspire or influence in these disconnected times ruled by the Churn, then you should build and maintain a diverse set of meaningful relationships. You need a relationship portfolio if you want to get big shit done. But here is the rub—it must be for the right reasons. The relationship must be the asset, not the means to a transaction. If you don't follow this simple biological reality, the other party will sniff you out and you'll lose trust at a critical moment.

We are remarkably similar in how we are wired to interact with one another. When that wiring shorts or overloads, it exposes us to the Churn. Maybe you had a bad day at work, maybe you felt unheard on that Zoom meeting, maybe you got rejected by a friend or passed over for a promotion. Your social hardwiring has been messed with and fear and anger have kicked in. And as we know, once you're afraid or pissed, you turn inward, becoming more asocial and disconnected—the trance.

You must fight this. When things fall apart, connection is everything. The next crisis is always right around the corner. To better deal with it, we need to get more deliberate, more intentional about our connections. We need to remember that the social aspect of our ingrained human nature is our superpower; it provides us with a competitive edge when everyone else is in survival mode. We need to embrace this superpower.

We also need to recognize that our ability to connect has been degraded to a critically low threshold by the Churn, and we must fight that degradation. We must double down on our social intentions.

This is a shift in mindset. Take a page from Jim Gant and

connect like your life depends on it. Because in the next crisis, it just might.

Managing Relationships Is a Team Sport

My first deployment as a young captain with a Green Beret detachment was to Colombia on a counternarcotics mission. I was cherry (new) as hell, and the strategic requirements that had been placed on our little team in that war-torn country felt personally overwhelming.

This sense of being in too deep was a mirage, though. I had failed to account for my team.

I quickly learned that my teammates—who had all been here before—had developed deep relationships with all kinds of people: senior Colombian officials, embassy employees, even local shopkeepers. My team sergeant introduced me to these people, explaining later that these relationships had been built over decades and had been passed from one team to the next. Together, they all worked to move the national security objectives of the United States downfield five yards at a time. I never forgot that.

Nobody wins alone. The Churn has created such a transactional approach to life that relationship management is largely based on money or power and little else. This just adds to our sense of "I'm in it for me" disconnection, since we're all reduced to individuals trying to extract money or clout from other individuals. Of course, the isolation brought on by the COVID pandemic—a society-wide isolation from which we will be recovering for years—only makes our disconnection worse.

I believe there's an urgent need for each of us to learn (or relearn) how to manage our relationships. Relationships are essential all the time but are crucial in hard times—especially relationships within and between organizations. We each have a role to play. In business, it can't just be the designated "relationship manager" or human resources department that is responsible for navigating the thickets of our social connections. This duty falls on the shoulders of everyone in a leadership position, from executive officers to individual team managers who oversee only a handful of people. Or from parents to older siblings. Or from the head coach to the assistant coaches to the team captains on the field. These organizational relationships must be treated like Fabergé eggs as they are passed gingerly from one person to the next and to the next. Eventually, they make a full circuit. It goes around, it comes around.

But if just one person slips up—if one person devalues a critical relationship—it shatters on the floor and you can kiss your precious, hard-earned social capital goodbye.

The Power of Bottom-Up

In the section "Surrender to Purpose," I mentioned the ad hoc program I led that helped rescue our Afghan allies. We named that effort Operation Pineapple Express. For several intense weeks in 2021, about 120 people, scattered all around the world, worked 24/7 to evacuate American citizens, Afghan commandos and special forces, interpreters, and even government officials and their families from Afghanistan before the country was handed over to the Taliban. Shamefully, the US government had abandoned these people and their families, making no effort or guarantee to move them to safety. If they remained, they were sure to be hunted down and killed by the Taliban. The American withdrawal from Afghanistan was botched in many respects, but this was one of the most glaring examples of our government dropping the ball. No one was coming to save our old friends and partners. Our top-down leadership had failed.

Which left Operation Pineapple Express and other volunteer groups to fill the breach.

In the end, we saved approximately one thousand Afghans. We couldn't save everybody, but we tried, and to a meaningful extent we succeeded where the behemoth US government couldn't. One of the men I was closest to throughout my time in Afghanistan—a wiry, resourceful, funny, and lethal young commando named Nezam—was able to escape to freedom. Today he lives in the United States with his young kids. I love him and I am so happy and relieved that he is safe.

How do we function, how do we lead, in situations like this? Why was a ragtag group of veterans, former intelligence professionals, nonprofit employees, and regular people able to succeed at what was essentially a rescue and recovery operation where the greatest operational and logistics conglomerate in the history of the world, the United States, had failed?

Because we worked from the bottom up.

In their seminal work *The Starfish and the Spider*, Ori Brafman and Rod Beckstrom introduce the concepts of "spider organizations" and "starfish organizations."

Spider organizations are traditional top-down organizations, like the US government. If the spider's head is cut off or paralyzed, the organization can't function. These organizations are defined by bureaucracy and chains of command. Their rigid structure stifles decision making and the ability to act quickly.

By contrast, starfish organizations are resilient, a bit incoherent, and bottom-up, like Operation Pineapple Express. They are officially leaderless. Like with a starfish, if one appendage is lost then another grows back, continuing to kick ass.

When tough challenges arise, I've learned that you can bring concerned members from spider and starfish organizations together from the bottom up. I call these types of organizations "communities of practice." They are composed of diverse members from different backgrounds who share a common purpose in an ecosystem focused on solving a wicked, ill-structured problem.

I first implemented a community of practice in Afghanistan in 2010 when we began doing Village Stability Operations. We were losing the war. Our wicked problem was stabilizing rural Afghan villages, places that were haunted by forty years of war and societal decay, intimidated by Taliban and other bad actors, detached from their top-down, corrupt government, and pressed upon by a complex suite of coalition forces and civilian agencies and NGOs.

Nearly every top-down effort to stabilize these villages had failed. But by working on the ground over the course of two years, using the techniques I now call Rooftop Leadership, we were able to achieve positive outcomes in areas of security, economic development, and governance. Our diverse group—Green Berets, diplomats, Afghan leaders, their friends and family members—came together around a set of common goals. Through herculean effort, we succeeded. (For a few years anyway, until the government shut the program down. But that's another story.)

I brought this same ethos to Operation Pineapple Express. We were a community of diverse individuals intent on helping our Afghan friends, and we were not going to fail. We leveraged our personal relationships and called in favors, and we worked until it was impossible to work any longer.

This kind of community of practice can be brought to bear on lots of different situations. Two years after Operation Pineapple Express, I received a desperate text from an old friend. We'll call him Brad.

Brad was deeply connected with Lahaina, Hawaii, which had been ravaged by a brutal wildfire in 2023. "Scott," he texted, "do you think you could help some of these folks get organized to deal with this horrible loss?"

Brad was tapping me not because I had any intimate knowledge of Hawaii or any deep connections to the people or leaders in this community, but because he knew that I could organize people quickly around a common goal. He understood that I knew how to put a community of practice into, well, practice.

(Not incidentally, I had a recent if brief connection to Lahaina. Monty, the boys, and I had spent a wonderful Christmas there in 2022. I have seen many devastated and ruined places, but I could hardly comprehend the level of loss this community had experienced, and the speed with which it had occurred.)

"I'm here to help," I texted back. I reached out to a few buddies from Operation Pineapple Express and a couple other local folks on the ground Brad had connected me to, and within minutes Task Force Lahaina was up and running.

One of the people in this community of practice was named Amy. She was a force of nature who led multiple nonprofits and volunteers. Along with Fox News host Will Cain, Amy helped fill a private cargo plane to deliver thousands of pounds of building materials, respirators, and medical gear to community leaders in Lahaina.

Other than getting the initial players connected, I had very little to do with the goodwill this group brought to bear on a terrible situation. I made the e-introductions and got out of the way.

I believe—no, I know—that these bottom-up community approaches are what is missing from today's leadership. I fully believe that it will be communities like these that pull us back from the abyss.

I know from experience that these communities are not homogeneous. They never are. This diversity is a technical advantage. You say, "We're so different." I say, "Good. Can we agree that this wicked problem needs to be solved? If so, then it's our diverse backgrounds that will give us power."

I'd like to shout out social media in this context. I've spilled a fair amount of ink against social media in these pages, but when it comes to communities of practice, social media, and even 24/7 news, can play an essential role. Professional platforms like LinkedIn and Signal enable a community of practice to maintain contact and exchange ideas. If we can resist the Churn of our digital entanglement, our digital tools give us an unprecedented ability to create effective communities of practice in the service of getting big shit done.

Build Trust When Risk Is Low

Operation Pineapple Express was successful because its volunteers had built social capital in lots of places and with lots of different people over the course of twenty-plus years. This process can be summed up very succinctly: Build trust when risk is low, leverage it when risk is high.

Unfortunately, we live in times of chaos and complexity. When things are relatively calm, we must build trust for the next pandemic, the next financial meltdown, the next war.

This process isn't always easy. The tempo of our mechanistic, left-brain, above-the-waterline world actively diminishes the importance of human connection. When "time is short" and "time is money," focusing on anything other than the bottom line can feel inconvenient and superfluous.

But as many leaders found out during the pandemic, this is a short-term attitude to a long-term ass kicking. Nobody is coming to save you—but going it alone is a fool's errand. Transactional relationships will be the first thing to fall away when life gets truly difficult.

Take a hard look at your relationships. All of them. Business relationships, friendships, familial relationships.

Taking the time to build trust and social capital when risk is low is how we will navigate the next crisis, whatever it happens to be.

Gratitude Never Goes Out of Style

Gratitude goes a long way, especially when times get tough. My fellow Green Berets taught me this. Whenever we deployed anywhere in the world, my team sergeant, Shawn, insisted on handing out these cheesy-ass Certificates of Appreciation to people who helped us. You know, the kind you'd get in summer camp, made of rigid construction paper in cheap black plastic frames. They said something like:

> This Certificate of Appreciation is presented to Capitan Delgar Fuentes for unmatched support to SFODA 726 while conducting joint special operations with the Colombian Commandos. Your professionalism resulted in an increased capability to defend the Colombian people. Your commitment and loyalty represent the highest level of credit upon you, your unit, and the entire Colombian Military.

Shawn and I would give these to every single organization and individual who helped us in any way. The armorer. The range NCO. The proprietor of the local pizzeria who fed us after long days on the range.

We would spend hours preparing and signing the damn things. It drove me crazy.

But on a mission to Paraguay, I learned my lesson. A recent coup attempt by a disgruntled general had almost overthrown the government. We were being sent in to train the nation's top commando unit so that any future coup attempts would also not succeed. Except I'd screwed up—I'd failed to secure the training area and we had nowhere to do our final training exercise.

This final exercise would demonstrate the combined arms power of Paraguayan special operations. It was a national exhibition. It was meant to send a strategic message to any insurgent holdouts thinking about future uprisings: "Don't even think about it." The top brass of the Paraguayan military would be there, as well as several US generals and the US ambassador. With no place to rehearse the exercise, this was a big screwup.

After I dropped the ball, my second in command arranged for me to have dinner with a well-connected Paraguayan Army officer. I had a big ask for him about getting access to the training range. I knew asking him to cancel other units from training in favor of our rehearsal could put his reputation with his peers at risk.

When I arrived at his home, he touched my elbow and led me around. When we got to his living room, I stopped cold. Every inch of every wall was decorated with these same certificates from my Special Forces Group, dating back to 1987.

The. Entire. Room.

I'll be honest, it was a little creepy. But boy did I get the point.

Each of those certificates was a down payment of social capital from some previous team that enabled me to make my big ask and get a positive answer. I got my training area without issue. Those simple pieces of paper and cheap plastic frames added up to a level of reciprocity I never could have otherwise expected. They contributed to a relationship that proved strategic when it mattered most.

The takeaway: Humans are social creatures. Gratitude never goes out of style. Neither does hospitality.

When you are building your communities of practice around common goals and purposes, ensure that you recognize good work with tangible gratitude and that you demonstrate hospitality to the people you serve. Don't do this because you expect something; do it because the relationship is an asset that you value.

The reciprocity that results can change lives, and maybe even save some.

Introductions Are Sacred

The caustic nature of the Churn makes bringing people into the fold around wicked problems more challenging than ever. Whether you are introducing a guest speaker, connecting a relevant prospect to your organization at a mixer, or welcoming a newcomer to your nonprofit on a Teams call, introductions are sacred.

We are social creatures who each struggle with the Churn and with the isolation that we experience in everyday life. The least little shift in emotional temperature or hint of a perceived slight can cause a critical participant to walk away from joining a strategic group or movement. We can't afford this when battling wicked problems. Somehow, we must bridge these initial connection gaps.

The ability to introduce people is *strategic*. Many leaders just blow this off. I can't tell you how many times I've cringed behind the curtain while the moderator of a conference reads my bio word for word. Or how many times I've sat in a video call to discuss a humanitarian effort when no one bothered to take the time to introduce everyone present.

Never forget: Introductions take practice, they require intention. Don't worry about how much time they take up. It's worth it.

The next time you introduce someone to an individual or a group, try this:

Meet with the new person ahead of time. Take a few minutes to ask thoughtful, open-ended questions. "How did you get into this nonprofit effort?" "What's the toughest challenge you've overcome that you'd like the audience to know about?" "What's the most profound thing you learned about yourself when your business got hit by the pandemic?"

Then just listen as they tell their story. You won't even have to take notes. If it's a story, you'll remember. We're hardwired for this.

When it comes time for you to make the actual introduction, just tell their story. (Make sure you get their permission beforehand.) Use their words to talk about why this person's story is important to you, and why you're connecting this person to the group. Sharing someone's story is an immediate trust accelerant, and it lays the foundation for reciprocity within the group. This is an advanced synthesis of active listening and human connection. It requires you to know what the audience values and the new person has to offer. This is the kind of thing most leaders don't do, especially senior or self-important leaders. But it provides a competitive edge for those who do take the time to get it right.

One more thing: e-introductions are just as sacred. They may even be *more* sacred since they are so impersonal.

I once had the privilege to work with General Stan McChrystal of Joint Special Operations Command. He was masterful at connecting diverse groups across the globe, and the stakes were always high. He was especially adept at e-introductions. Whether over video or email, he always opened with an authentic greeting, no matter how junior or senior the new person was. He would never move on until this introduction was complete.

By prioritizing human connection, even in the digital realm, General McChrystal was able to bring people along quickly and effectively.

When you're making an e-connection, it's critical to remember that just handing someone an email address or a phone number is *not* a connection. You must go further.

I suggest something like this:

Dear Samantha,

I hope this note finds you and your family well. It hasn't been the same since you left for the new job but I'm sure you're crushing it.

Samantha, please meet my friend Ruth. She's an old-school advocate for veterans and their families. She just moved to the area and reached out to me. She's got some great connections and wants to jump right in. I immediately thought of you.

Ruth, not only is Samantha an old friend but she's also leading the charge on veteran transition in the Tampa Bay area. She's got a lot of time in the saddle and she can bring you up to speed easily.

Oh, and you're both Marines so I know that will get you off to a great start.

Samantha, meet Ruth. Ruth, meet Samantha.

I'll leave it there and get out of the way. So glad you're connected now.

> Best,
> Scott

This same practice applies to video and conference calls. Don't proceed with the agenda until everyone has been introduced. If there are too many folks for that, then try saying something like, "Before we start, let's review who's in the room." And then introduce each person briefly but with intention. If these basic introductions aren't made, then "digital butt sniffing" will dominate the meeting. People will break into tribal side chats, surf the internet, or make up false stories in their heads about certain people in the meeting. Not only does this erode your collective ability to get shit done, but it also undermines trust and undercuts social capital.

When it comes to introductions, amateurs get right to the bottom line. Professionals connect first, and then they move on.

The Decisive Point

In military planning there's a concept called the "decisive point." This is a critical component of any operation that focuses the energy and actions of the involved parties on a particular point in time and space. For example, if we were planning a mission to rescue a noncombatant who'd been taken away to an enemy encampment, we might name the emplacement of our sniper overwatch team as the decisive point.

If that sniper team can get set up without being detected, then we've achieved a tactical advantage before the raid even commences.

We've already started to win. It's decisive.

There is a decisive point in every human interaction. It's the point when the other party becomes ready to hear what you have to say. It's when they become open to listening.

"What will it take to help the other person get ready to hear what I have to say?" is a question I try to ask myself before any interaction.

Because it's decisive.

Go Local or Go Home

Living in Afghan villages taught me something that living on a firebase didn't. Context is everything. Local is the most relevant.

Yet because of our entanglement with the digital domain, context is usually the first thing to go. A car chase on the other side of the country or the ongoing mystery of a missing person that gets reported every few minutes puts us in a trance and holds our attention. But they offer no context. This means it's impossible for us to be relevant to the situation. We are merely unwitting cogs in the Matrix.

We can't allow that to happen.

We must fight for context—*always*.

When we first started the Village Stability Operations in Afghanistan, I was called out one day to witness a very bizarre sight. Young villagers were squatting in the freshly tilled fields smashing fat earthworms with their thumbs.

I stared openmouthed next to a Green Beret captain I'll call Jeremy. "What the hell are they doing?" I asked. Every farmer around the world knows that earthworms are critical to soil health.

"They think the worms eat the crops," Jeremy said, just as flabbergasted.

Then we started talking to them and getting some context. We soon learned that these men had spent most of their lives in refugee camps in Pakistan. They had never farmed. Their parents had farmed, but most of them were dead or in hiding. Since knowledge was handed down orally in their society, there was no way for them to know that earthworms were a good thing.

For the previous ten years, as we kicked in doors on missions launched from built-up firebases, we'd had no idea how damaged the fabric of informal Afghan civil society had become. Only when we knelt in the plowed fields beside them or listened intently to stories in their Jirga councils did we learn the truth about their local reality. Now, we had a good idea about how to be more relevant, about how we could better serve them. In time, we showed them through model farms that worms were a good thing—a necessary thing—for farming. That year's crop was so bountiful that compelling these men to come up on the rooftop and fight alongside us was relatively easy.

The same holds in our complex, fast-paced world where we treat each other with indifference, contempt, and moral superiority, usually because we don't understand where other people are coming from. Meet people where they are, not where we want them to be. When we go local and find out why the other side is killing earthworms, shared perspective starts to open doors to new opportunities.

Context is everything. And to gain it, you must go local or go home.

Empathetic Witness

In this time of Churn, we don't trust leaders who sit in their ivory towers and prescribe solutions to the masses through faceless, uninformed bureaucratic policies and their strategic comms machine.

Why should we? They don't reflect the pain we feel in our daily existence, and they're not relevant to the things we value in our lives or work.

For example, any manager can bark orders. But people don't want to be yelled at. And when things are stressful, they definitely don't like to be told what to do. They do like being reminded about what's important. Including themselves.

There is a pathway to relevance. Be an *empathetic witness*.[18]

This one is simple. It means exactly what it says.

It's about serving the people you lead. It means leaving our ivory towers and getting down in the trenches. Not for a photo op or a check-the-block walkabout. Your people will smell it on you, and it will create even more distrust.

I'm talking about being with your people for the sake of pure discovery. For bearing witness to the people you serve, and the burdens they carry. Don't judge them. Don't criticize. Simply walk around and strive to see the pictures in their heads. Relate to their pain. Be relevant to their goals.

Being an empathetic witness doesn't mean you have to hold the answers to their problems. You likely won't. Don't get me wrong—if you see something wrong, correct it. If there is a problem, call it out. I'm not diminishing the need for a chain of command and issuing directives. But within that context of a divisive Churn and getting big shit done, you must bear witness to what's happening at a human level. You'll ask about their personal journeys, professional perspective, and you'll listen. When people sense that you're authentic and that you're acting with intention, the armor plates fall away, and people become ready for what you have to say. You've reached the decisive point, together.

And you have been rewarded with the competitive advantage all good leaders crave most: context.

Intention and Discovery

When you show up with intention, people pay attention. You instantly become more relatable to the people you serve.

But as we all know, showing up with intention can seem awfully rare. People entranced by the Churn usually treat other people as inconveniences. Everything is "right now" and "get it done." So many of our interactions are transactional, short-form communications that do more to drive us apart than bring us together.

If leadership is managing energy, then before we interact with others, we should set our intentions. And the root of these should be *discovery*.

Green Berets taught me that preparation is two-thirds of every successful interaction. We must get clear on who we're dealing with, what they value, what their pain is centered on.

We also must prepare ourselves. High stakes can freak us out. We look like we don't trust ourselves. Which makes it harder for others to trust us. We must get into the appropriate emotional temperature for the interaction at hand. In fact, this is the first thing we must do. When possible, it even involves preparing the physical space of our interaction. Preparation is how we manage our emotional temperature and establish our intention with the other party.

How many times do people show up to meetings completely unprepared, uninterested, or even annoyed? Their intention is on themselves, on what just happened on their conference call, or on what they are planning to say to their Realtor when they get home. They are not present. And when you're not present, you don't appear trustworthy.

The secret to a successful interaction, no matter if it's with a total stranger or the president of the United States, is to show up with an intention 100 percent built around discovery.

Discovery of the pictures in their head and nothing else.

What are those pictures? Pain and goals.

No agenda. No past. No future.

Just discovery.

The other party will sense this and the dance of authentic connection will begin. From there, the storytelling can commence.

CHAPTER 7

Storytelling

or, The Engine of Hope

The most powerful person in the world is the storyteller.
The storyteller sets the vision, values, and agenda of an
entire generation that is to come.

—Steve Jobs

Welcome to Stay In Step

Not long after returning from my second combat tour, I learned
that one of my oldest friends, Chief Warrant Officer Romulo
"Romy" Camargo, had been shot through the neck while lead-
ing a combat patrol in Afghanistan. Romy was one of the finest
Green Berets I'd ever worked with, and I was devastated. (No
matter how many friends of yours get shot or blown up, you
never get used to it.) He was just about to land in Washington,

DC, where doctors at Walter Reed Medical Center would attempt a last-ditch surgery to save his life. I was working in DC at the time. I could be at the hospital within minutes.

Romy survived the surgery. Afterward, he was moved from Walter Reed to the James A. Haley VA Hospital in Tampa. He was paralyzed from the shoulders down and ventilator dependent. Some doctors cautioned that Romy might never leave the VA hospital. But they were wrong.

Romy and his wife, Gaby, moved into a specially modified house in Tampa, and he soon received a special exemption to travel to Portugal to undergo cutting-edge stem cell therapy. When he returned to the United States, Romy needed aggressive rehabilitation for his spinal cord injury (SCI), especially with load-bearing exercises, weights, and trainers. The only place he could do this was at a rehab center in Orlando, which was eighty-five miles from Tampa—an hour-and-a-half drive each way. But he and Gaby banded together and did it, two or three times a week, month after month, year after year.

Five years after Romy's injury, I sat across from him and Gaby at their kitchen table. They wanted to discuss something. I just felt blessed to be there. They were the true definition of "power couple."

"It's time for a new chapter, Scott," Gaby said.

Romy no longer breathed automatically like you and I do. Every night, he slept with a ventilator, and whenever he was awake, he had to consciously breathe, taking short sips of air.

This was most noticeable whenever he spoke. "We have an idea...brother...but we need your help," Romy said, taking three stabs of breath to get the words out.

"What is it?" I asked, a knot of anticipation forming in my stomach.

"I'll be medically...retired in a few months," Romy said. "I've come far...but I won't be able...to go to Orlando...for workouts anymore."

"The drive is too much," Gaby added. "It's too much for any Tampa-based spinal cord patient, and there are dozens of them around here. There's no place for them to go." I could hear the excitement growing in her voice.

"Gaby and I know...this recovery regimen...inside and out...We can do this."

I didn't understand. "Do what?"

Gaby grinned. "We want to open our own SCI recovery center right here in Tampa."

"'Stay In Step'...We want you to be...our chairman of the board...Scott," Romy said intensely.

"Chairman? Is there a board?"

Romy looked around the table. "There's us, so...yeah."

I shook my head and threw up my hands. "Okay. You know I'm in," I said. We hugged tightly and agreed to start the next day. On the drive home, I thought about what I had agreed to. I didn't want to fail them, but I wasn't sure we could pull it off.

About a year later, we had a five-person board and—not much else. Raising money for a rehab center had turned out to be no easy task. None of us knew what we were doing. We held fundraisers. We held raffles. We went door to door. We flew Romy to events when it seemed appropriate. But it wasn't enough.

We had also rented a space. A five-thousand-square-foot mess in an industrial park. Ceiling tiles were missing. Wires and HVAC ducts dangled from above. The walls were banged up and dented, and half the floor had been torn up. We had no equipment, and no money to start the remodel. Rent for the space was coming due, and cash was low.

Then we heard from Lieutenant General Martin Steele, one of our board members. He was very tapped into the corporate world. He told us that a senior executive from Toyota named Simon Nagata was in South Florida and wanted to meet with veterans. He had an open slot in his schedule that same day, and General Steele wanted him to meet Romy. "This could be big," General Steele said. "But you'll have to hustle."

It was on.

I insisted that we take Mr. Nagata through our run-down space instead of showing him our PowerPoint and walking him through numbers and charts. I felt that we needed to connect with him on a personal level. General Steele didn't favor this idea, mainly because the space was so crappy. But I believed this was the only way to win Toyota's support.

I waited outside. My phone rang. It was General Steele. "We'll be there in five minutes. I hope you're right about this."

Two minutes later, a fleet of eight Toyota minivans rolled up. As I waited for the doors to open, I glanced back at the facility to give a thumbs-up to Romy and Gaby. It suddenly hit me that we didn't even have a sign for our would-be rehab center. That was probably an oversight. *Damn*, I thought. *Oh well. Too late now.*

Mr. Nagata wasn't hard to spot. He was in his sixties, had a stern demeanor, and wore a perfectly pressed suit. He walked up to me and shook my outstretched hand without smiling or saying a word. General Steele gave me a strained smile. Mr. Nagata's entourage brushed past me without a peep and entered the building. I trailed behind, suddenly certain I'd given Romy and Gaby bad advice.

When I finally entered, my blood turned cold. Mr. Nagata stood in the center of the dusty room with a scowl that would have peeled paint from the walls—if they had actually been painted. He glared at me. He looked down at Romy in his wheelchair. Then he went back to glowering at the dingy yellow walls. He was quite obviously thinking, *What the hell is this place and why am I here?*

Then Gaby swooped in. "Hello. My name is Gabriella Camargo, but you can call me Gaby," she said. "Mr. Nagata, welcome to Stay In Step." She asked him some questions about his family and his understanding of spinal cord injuries. As he spoke, she took his arm and gently moved him around the facility. When he stopped speaking, she began telling him about Stay In Step.

"Over here is where our physical therapists and trainers will be working with our clients," she said. "We will have state-of-the-art equipment. We're going to help people like my husband, Romy. He's the inspiration for all of us." Mr. Nagata looked at him and nodded. "He can't shake your hand, but he likes it when you give his hand a little squeeze." Gaby waited. Mr. Nagata did as she suggested.

Romy smiled. "Pleased to...meet you...sir."

"Romy will be right here on this floor with our trainers," Gaby said, "exercising and encouraging our clients to work hard. It's very important that we push their comfort zone in these workouts."

"Why do you require such demanding exercises for people who are paralyzed?" Mr. Nagata asked.

"Because the current protocol for spinal patients is substandard," Gaby explained. "Their bodies atrophy and they tend to die much sooner than they should. We don't accept that here at Stay In Step," she said, as if the place already existed. "We believe in hard work and creating a quality of life that no other rehab facility offers."

Mr. Nagata raised an eyebrow and nodded.

Gaby didn't waste any time. She hooked his arm and led him to the other side of the facility. "This will be the family room. Spinal cord injuries affect the entire family, not just the one in recovery. The burdens on caregivers are massive. We will have a comfortable couch for the family members to rest on and to visit with each other. And maybe even a massage chair."

She kept going.

"And this will be the children's room, Mr. Nagata." She took a moment to compose herself. "Our son, Andres, was eighteen months old when Romy was injured. We spent five months in Walter Reed Hospital. Andres had to play on the toilet in Romy's room because that was all he had." She threw her shoulders back defiantly and raised her index finger. "That will *never* happen at Stay In Step. Our children will have the chance to be kids while they're here. They'll have fun."

Mr. Nagata didn't move; his stony face betrayed no emotion. But then, I saw it. When he turned to face Gaby, a tear ran down his face.

"I'm going to help you," he finally said. He turned to Romy and repeated, "I'm going to help you." Then he bowed, waved at his entourage, and left. I followed them outside and watched the parade of minivans drive away as quickly as they had arrived. I went back inside to Romy and Gaby. The three of us had no idea what had just happened, but we felt it.

Something had changed.

Three weeks later, General Steele called. "Scott, are you ready for this? Nagata and Toyota are donating $250,000! Stay

In Step is open for business, buddy!" I have a lot of fond memories from being around the military community, but one of the finest of all was Romy's and Gaby's expressions when I told them the good news.

The opening ceremony took place two months later in the sweltering Tampa heat. I was master of ceremonies. Mr. Nagata gave the keynote. Gaby and Romy cut the ribbon. Above the entrance, the sign—yes, we now had a sign—read *Stay In Step*, complete with a Toyota logo in the corner. More than a dozen beaming spinal cord injury patients sat in their wheelchairs in the front row. Inside, the family room had that massage chair, and the kids' room was painted in bright colors and was full of books and toys. It was just like she'd told in her story to Mr. Nagata.

A story that had come true. Welcome to Stay In Step.*

The Power of Narrative Competence

Humans are story animals. In fact, our brain is a metaphorical, pattern-matching organ.[19] We are wired to hear, deliver, and comprehend stories. They are how we make meaning of the world around us; they are how we have made meaning of

---

*If you'd like to learn more about the amazing story and mission of Gaby and Romy Camargo and the awe-inspiring Stay In Step community, you can check them out at stayinstep.org.

the world for tens of thousands of years. For the brain to build new patterns, it needs new stories. As meaning-seeking and meaning-assigning creatures, this can't be understated.

Our right brain understands narrative. Our left brain does not. In fact, our left brain rejects narratives and opts for data and contextless summaries meant to fill the gaps of the sketchy, re-presented virtual realm it holds so dear.

Think about it. You see it all around. Everything is a bullet point or a soundbite or an Instagram post.

Yet our ancient thirst for storytelling remains unquenched. I believe that the exhausted majority is desperate for storytelling. I've been on thousands of stages in the public and private sectors, and storytelling shows up as a welcome relief every time. It never gets old. You don't believe me? Ask Taylor Swift. Ask Chris Stapleton. Ask Drake. Ask their millions upon millions of fans. Better yet...ask Gaby.

Let's start by defining a few key terms: *Story* is defined as a detailed narration of a character's struggles to overcome obstacles and reach an important goal.[20] But what about putting the story out into the world? The Rooftop Leadership definition of *storytelling* is the transfer of relevant imagery from one human to another. Storytelling has an additional Rooftop component, which I call "narrative competence."

This is defined as purposeful, goal-oriented storytelling in real time. This is where the rubber meets the road for authentic influence. The "real time" aspect is key. The ability to use storytelling in dynamic, unpredictable situations is an elite skill. Narrative competence can be used when giving a keynote to a room full of donors. It can be used when recording a hasty voice memo to a Signal chat room when lives are on the line. It can be one-on-one with a client. Gaby demonstrated expert narrative competence when she took Mr. Nagata's arm and walked him around Stay In Step before it was actually Stay In Step. He left with new patterns in his brain and a determination to lend a hand.

Having narrative competence, and using it, will help you get shit done when no one is coming, but it takes practice.

When the stakes are high, is it worth it to lead with story?

Just ask the hundreds of clients with spinal cord injuries who have received life-changing therapy from Stay In Step.

Busting the Myth of "Bedtime Stories"

Sadly, too many people don't see it this way. They say, "Time is money," and they can't get past that.

Not too long ago, the leader of a large tech company asked me, "Why do we need to mess with bedtime stories when our company is hemorrhaging money?" Needless to say, he lacked the trust of his own people and struggled to connect with prospects and clients.

Here's what I told him: "They're not bedtime stories, they're how we understand each other. There's a real and tangible return on investment to learning how to lead with story. It's deep work, work that will help you and your company meet your goals."

I wasn't sure he'd heard me until he shared his backstory of mental health challenges at a leadership conference, inspiring the entire room.

Stories provide meaning, context, emotional connection, and are remembered for a long time. Some of this reads like other material in this book, and there is some crossover, but there are also differences that are essential for narrative competence. Let's explore each value proposition for storytelling.

Meaning. Humans have a neurological mandate to make sense of the world. We crave meaning. Information comes to us through our senses, which is processed into metaphor and image in our huge prefrontal cortex. I've written derisively about the "trance state" foisted upon us by our disconnected, tech-heavy world, but the fact is that the brain prefers trance states. In a very real sense, reality is a shared trance that we happen to agree on. Stories take advantage of this. They create a trance state in the listener that allows them to open and to deeply focus on what you have to say. Storytelling enables listeners to locate themselves in your story, which gives them...

Context. We live in a complex world with wicked, ill-structured problems. Stories cut through complexity. Because the brain works in metaphor, stories allow the audience to develop context around these wicked problems. As we discussed in the previous section, without context we have no hope of making or maintaining...

Emotional connection. We're always trying to figure out who we can trust and who we can't. Well-told, authentic stories establish trust. They are the fast track to trust. Stories make emotional connections across race, religion, and politics. Our deep biological appreciation of stories often creates reciprocity. After hearing a good story from an authentic teller, people are more open to meeting and helping the teller. One prime reason for this is that well-told stories are immediately stored in our...

Long-term memory. On several occasions I've taught senior Green Berets about managing and executing high-stakes engagements. On one such teaching trip, the major who'd invited me had been a student of mine, as a young captain, during the Green Beret Qualification Course. At one point, I asked him to leave the room. I told the remaining Green Berets the story about meeting Mark in the Mount Ida soda shop when I was a kid. Then I asked the major to come back and recount what my age had been from the same story, which I had told him four years earlier and not since. His soldiers were stunned when he said, "Fourteen," without any hesitation. Point being: People remember your stories long after you are gone.

If I'm training Green Berets who are about to deploy into a low-trust, dangerous environment, and I only have time to teach either tactics for close-quarters combat or narrative competence, I'll teach the latter.

Every damn time.

Resistance to Storytelling

People are reluctant to tell their own stories. Whether I'm working with Navy SEALs in transition or mid-level corporate leaders, I hear three consistent objections:

"Nobody wants to hear my story."

"I don't have a story."

"My story isn't as good as her story."

These are forms of what bestselling self-help expert Steven Pressfield calls "Resistance." These are negative internal voices that hold us down. Resistance is a form of self-sabotage that our left brain drives relentlessly.

There are some very simple answers to these resistance-fueled storytelling killers:

"Nobody wants to hear my story." A simple, bald-faced lie we tell ourselves. People are relieved when they're told a story. But you can't be casual about it. You need to commit to it, and build your narrative muscles, or the Churn and its distracted minions will eat you alive. Or, at minimum, ignore you.

"I don't have a story." Another left-brain lie. We are story animals. Every moment, every event in your life is converted into a story by your ancient brain. So, you are right, you don't have a story...you have tens of thousands of stories.

"My story isn't as good as her story." Storytelling isn't a competition. If you tell a story that means something to you, in all likelihood it will mean something to me. Beware of the desire to prejudge or self-edit your story when bringing it into the world. Stay the course. Fight for it. It literally has the potential to change someone's life—including your own.

And Yet—It's Not About You

One evening, when my friend and mentor Bo Eason was touring the country and putting on his play, his mom and brother decided to attend. Bo was horrified. The play told some tough stories about his family and the challenges they had faced, challenges he'd never discussed with either of them.

Seeing that this was on Bo's mind, and that he was in danger of pulling back, his director, Larry Moss, pulled him aside before the curtain went up. "Bo, I know your family is out there. But you need to forget about that. It's not about them. It's not even about you. It's about the story."

It's not about you, even when you are the protagonist. Stories are told in the service of others. So, the sooner you can get out of our own way in the service of the story, the better.

Go for the Ride

As I wrote earlier, storytelling is the transfer of imagery from one human to another.

Think about stories you heard when you were a kid. My grandpa ("Papa") would tell my cousins and me tales of hunting black bears in the Appalachian Mountains when he was a kid. As the fire popped and the smoke wafted upward, we'd get lost in a trance state as we ran barefoot alongside a transformed fifteen-year-old Papa through those dark mountain valleys. I can still see it in my mind.

That's narrative transportation. And it's a big payoff for the listener.

When a storyteller shares sensory details like what the air smelled like or what their stomach felt like when a pivotal moment happened, we experience it too. We are immediately transported into the narrative as we slip into a parasympathetic trance state. This two-sided ability—to both conjure the trance and receive it—is in our DNA. When it's done with expertise, we don't just appreciate the protagonist, we *become* the protagonist. We're able to take meaning from the story as if it were our own lived experience.

Whether it's a one-on-one session with your teenager about the dangers of addiction or a keynote to a corporate audience, narrative transportation creates a deep level of psychological safety and reciprocity that the insidiousness of the Churn cannot match. It is one of our best tools for breaking through. Storytelling is a warrior for that most intractable of human dispositions: hope.

The Engines of Hope

With so many divisive interactions in our polarized times, it's no wonder that we have such a massive exhausted majority. The divisionist leveraging of tribal behavior through the use of digital technology is enough to wear anyone down.

When members of the exhausted majority are afraid or angry, their brains navigate the Churn using old neuro-story maps from times when they previously experienced pain. In other words, their brains are telling them old stories to keep them from getting hurt again.

This can elicit all kinds of disconnection from our natural world and one another. We withdraw. We become hopeless.

It doesn't have to be this way.

Ben and Jess Owen stomp through the streets of South Memphis spreading hope. Both are recovering addicts who almost died in the trap houses of Melrose Street years ago. Now, they are clean and helping veterans and trafficked women and kids. They mobilize hundreds of thousands of people to raise money and buy back the trap houses where they almost died, and then turn these into halfway homes for addicts and trafficked victims.

How do they do this?

Storytelling.

More accurately, they use narrative competence to instill something in the exhausted majority that today's divisionist leaders simply can't generate.

Hope.

Their hope is more about what we share in common than what makes us different. Their hope is about self-actualization in the face of fear. Their hope is about better days for everyone. Because if they can help the kinds of people that everyone else has given up on, then there is hope for the rest of us.

Ben and Jess tell their stories of their own journeys to hell and back. What you're left with is not despair, it's hope. Or as Ben likes to say, "We turn dope houses into hope houses."

That's all the grist for the mill that you need. Tell your stories because they are the engines of hope.

It's Hard to Hate the Storyteller

Following a performance of *Last Out* in Washington, DC, we had a Q-and-A with the audience. A woman I'll call Claire stood up and said through tears, "I grew up in Northern Ireland. I saw constant violence and my memories of soldiers are dominated by trauma and fear. Since then, I've always had disdain for soldiers. But now, after seeing this play, I have a completely different view of soldiers. One of grace."

I was floored. The entire audience was, Claire included.

Here was a woman who had spent her childhood in fear of soldiers and her adult life resenting them. In under two hours, her entire viewpoint had shifted.

In this time of Churn, when divisionists, corporate news outlets, and social media divide us into tribes and factions for their own financial gain, storytelling builds bridges over religion, race, and politics toward shared perspectives.

The takeaway: It's hard to hate the storyteller. Telling your story can be scary, but don't worry. People won't hate you for it. They'll root for you.

Your Story Arsenal

I'm often asked, "Scott, I understand that storytelling is important, but what kind of stories should I tell when I'm just trying to get through the day?" Below is a breakdown of stories that will help you level up your narrative competence. There are other types of stories, but this is a good start.

Backstory. This is the story that gives people a sense of who you are. When you demonstrate narrative competence with your backstory, people choose *you* long before they choose your *idea* or *message*. Your backstory gives people the best sense of who you are in eight minutes or fewer. When people get a sense of who you are, they get a better sense of themselves, and the stage is set for them to be ready to listen (the narrative "decisive point").

Organizational story. This is the story about your organization that incorporates your collective purpose and what you're building together. Everyone on your team needs to help craft this story and should be able to tell it when you aren't around. You know you've succeeded when the people who work for and with you can tell the organizational story better than you can.

Not-your-success story. This is a kind of story that places the audience at the center. You share the journey of a third party, through hardship, and show how they met their goals. They are the hero; you are the guide. Because the audience identifies with stories autobiographically, they will likely locate themselves in your narrative. They will see themselves as the protagonist. This will help them make meaning in their own life and get a better sense of what it would be like to work with you.

Introduction story. As I wrote in an earlier section, introductions are sacred. The only thing sweeter than someone hearing their name spoken out loud is when another person tells their story better than they can. Again, make sure to get their permission first, but using stories to introduce people is powerful stuff. Get this one right, and you will accelerate trust on all sides.

Recognition story. How many chances do you get to honor the people you serve? If you're honest, you get a lot of chances. But do you take them? You should. Newcomers join your business. Team members depart for different assignments. Donors step up to support your community of practice. With just a little bit of planning, prior engagement, and a couple of thoughtful open-ended questions, you can tell the story of the person you are recognizing in the presence of others. While they proudly stand at your shoulder, you tap into a primal form of status and honor that gets the serotonin and reciprocity flowing. And yes, it works on Zoom as well. Recognizing others, just like introductions, is a sacred act. Don't screw it up by reading from a script.

Vision story. Several studies have shown that strategic leaders from Alexander the Great to Dr. Martin Luther King Jr. possessed two things: vision and a personal story to convey that vision. If your backstory is the narrative that gives us a sense of who you are, then your vision story is the narrative of what you are building and how the rest of us can help you build it. Gaby gave Mr. Nagata a vision story. Here's a tip: When you share your vision story, end by saying something like, "This isn't unique to me." You can then pivot the audience into the protagonist role and they will see *themselves* as the hero in your story. Otherwise, it's just about you, and nobody will help.

The Hero's Journey

Perhaps the best-known type of story is what's known as "the Hero's Journey." Odysseus, Gilgamesh, Robinson Crusoe, Ahab, Pinocchio, Victor Frankenstein, Huck Finn, Jay Gatsby,

Dorothy, Luke Skywalker, Malcolm X, Katniss Everdeen—all of these are characters (and at least one real person) whom we have followed, loved, rooted for (and occasionally against) in some of the most famous stories of all time. Their tales follow an established structure, marvelously explored by Joseph Campbell in his legendary book *The Hero with a Thousand Faces*.

I like this framework because it's universal; it will be the primary framework for many of the stories you tell. There's a certain internal logic to the Hero's Journey that will make perfect, almost intrinsic sense to you. Because—you guessed it—we're hardwired for it.

Here's my modified version, with a special shout-out not only to Joseph Campbell but also to my friend Steven Pressfield:

1. The hero hears a call.
2. The hero refuses the call.
3. The hero meets a guide.
4. The hero reluctantly answers the call.
5. The hero leaves the ordinary world and goes on a journey.
6. The hero ends up in the belly of the whale, facing struggles that are internal, external, or both.
7. The hero emerges from the struggle and returns home with a gift for the people.

Learn this framework, or better yet, build your own personal backstory using this framework, and you'll be off to the races. If you get stuck, head down to the bookstore or the library and pick up one of the classics. You won't regret it.

Pivotal Moments

Stories are built around moments.

The moment you first held your baby girl. The moment you found out you were having a baby girl. The moment you gave her away at the altar.

Moments.

There is a universality around them that is essential to narrative competence.

Pivotal moments—the really important moments—are even more essential to purposeful storytelling. These are the moments that changed the trajectory of your life. It might be the moment you heeded the call of the universe. It might be when you stepped out from cover and took a bullet. It might be when you saw no way out and went into your closet to fetch your gun, intent on using it on yourself.

It might be when your middle son came home and made you realize you were about to make the worst decision of your life.

This last moment is a perfect example of a pivotal moment. There is absolutely nothing remarkable about one of my boys walking through the front door making a shit ton of noise.

Nothing. It meant nothing to him or the friends he was with. But for me—it meant everything. It was *pivotal*.

Other moments that have defined my life: when Mark, the Green Beret, walked into the Mount Ida Soda shop and I asked him all those questions; when my Afghan friend Nezam called me and said he didn't want to die alone; when the lights came up on me for my first performance of *Last Out*.

Our ability to harvest pivotal moments and build stories around them is a critical skill. Catalog them, keep them close, don't forget them. Journal them. Build an archive of pivotal moments. They are timeless, and they will serve for as long as you live.

A Gift for the People

There are certain components that must be present in every story you tell, or you'll lose your audience. Struggle is a big one, but we'll save that for the next section of this book, since struggle is the final S of MESSS.

Resolution is another. How many times has someone told you a story only to leave you hanging? How many movies have you watched where the ending is, well, open-ended? How do you feel when this happens?

Most likely you're frustrated, maybe you're even angry. We need to know how a story ends so that we can extract the most meaning from it. If we don't know how it ends, then it's just about the teller and it's little more than a self-serving speech. God knows the world is too full of those...

Resolution is the "gift for the people" referred to in the Hero's Journey framework. Here are three essential components of resolution:

What happened. Sounds simple, but damn if it isn't overlooked all the time. The stories you tell are about a character (sometimes you, often someone else) trying to meet a goal. The character overcomes obstacles to do so. What happened along the way? Did they achieve their goal or not? Either way is fine. Life is full of stories that end badly. But we have to know, with clarity, how it ends in relation to the character and her goal.

Change. Life is about change. Movement and meaning are linked. Stasis is for amateurs, especially in this time of Churn. The brain is a sense-making tool, and it needs to know how the character changed as a result of the journey.

What was learned. Meaning can often be implicit in storytelling, but sometimes it's important to state things plainly. When I tell my story of becoming a Green Beret, I'm very explicit in describing that the journey was worth it because I learned how to read people, how to connect with other human beings, and how to move people to actions that they otherwise wouldn't take. That granular description of learning bridges the civil-military divide and sets me up to teach others those same skills in their own world, whatever it may be.

A good question to consider when crafting your story is: *What do I want my audience to feel when my story is over? What do I want them thinking about after I'm gone?* If you can answer these satisfactorily, you will have gone a long way in making certain your story serves your audience in the best possible way.

Storytelling 301

I've watched storytellers from indigenous cultures from all over the world share tales around a campfire. Some don animal skins and imitate the beasts they revere, some invoke the smoke from the fire, some call the spirits from other worlds; all of them commit their entire body to the storytelling effort, using physical gestures and pantomime. It's a performance. The listeners slip into a trance (the good kind) and sway to and fro, they gasp and holler as the storyteller transports them into their narrative universe.

Storytelling, in its most primal form, is a physical act.

The same should hold true for storytelling today, but too often it doesn't. Narrative competence—especially for people who aren't actors—is more than just writing down a powerful story. According to one study, human engagement is 60 percent physical, 30 percent vocal tone, and only 10 percent verbal.[21] Considering that storytelling has been around for as long as we've been human, and written language has only been around for about ten thousand years, this makes perfect sense.

Physical storytelling is all about casting a spell. When you do it well, it makes it impossible for your audience to do anything except fixate on you. Phones. Are. Down.

This is art and science. It's a craft of treating the body as a storytelling instrument that must be cleared of tension. Whether it is a keynote or a presentation, the instrument must be fully available for the delivery of the story. The body must breathe with intention, and it must be ready to access the storyteller's emotional reserves without hesitation.

This genuine emotional availability is the polar opposite of the speeches of perma-grin politicians hiding behind podiums, the talking points of corporate associates reciting techno-jargon PowerPoint slides from the neck up, or the networking of conference attendees speaking entire sentences in acronyms.

All of these "communicators" are unwatchable. Their habits and demeanor make us trust our "leaders" even less than we already do.

When you tell your story, make sure you integrate your body, your voice, and your spirit in the telling. Prepare. Commit fully. Manage your breath and allow your emotions to blow in and out like the wind.

This is storytelling 301. It's a physical act and the highest form of service. It takes practice.

A Relationship with Practice

Good storytellers own every room they walk into. Not in a sleazy way. They are relevant and—more important—they are relatable. We can't divert our eyes from them as they connect with us through narrative. It's not luck. They are not gifted. They work at it. Hard.

I always get a kick when people tell me how "lucky" I am to be able to get onstage or go on television to tell my story and make clear points. The truth is, I'm about to throw up in my mouth every time I get in front of people. My instincts tell me to get the hell off the stage. Instead, I work at it, breathe through it, and go out there.

In our time of Churn, you can't get by on instinct alone. Most people you'll get in front of are severely distracted and skeptical of anything and everything. Their attention span is measured in seconds, not minutes. Forget about an hour of undivided attention. You'll have to work your ass off to gain and hold their attention for the first thirty seconds. Lose your intention for just a moment, and they are gone, back into their phones. That causes you to feel anxiety and stage fright, which comes across in your demeanor, which drives more people to the exits—both figurative and literal.

You must train. This rule is inviolable.

And yet, I've seen veterans, for example, moving into civilian life violate this rule all the time. They think that because they've lived through dramatic, life-threatening experiences that they will automatically be able to hold a room with storytelling.

Maybe—but probably not.

The experience you gained on the battlefield in your own Hero's Journey exists within you. It has the potential to serve others, but you must metabolize it and bring it into the world in such a way that it is compelling and aligned with your entire being.

You must practice.

If you share a pivotal moment from your life in the service of others, it will likely involve some level of struggle, trauma, or emotion. Your body will try to lock down and stop right when you need to keep going. It's fight, flight, or freeze. To get past this, you must do reps, just like with any other learned skill. Your body is your instrument. You must integrate your story with your body so that it grows accustomed to it. Once you do, it will flow as freely as a mountain stream.

This isn't just an issue for veterans. Civilian leaders in the public and private sectors also violate the practice principle when it comes to storytelling. They often think that because they're high on the food chain, all they must do to prepare for the all-hands meeting is review their seventy-five slides before the meeting begins. Nope. Your audience will check their phone just as quickly when you are a CEO boring the shit out of them as they would with a ho-hum coworker.

They'll just be a bit more careful about it.

The Stories We Ask to Hear

I felt like giving up. Our unit had been trying to get into this contentious Afghan village to conduct Village Stability Operations for months. There was no support from the elders. Most of them sat stoic and offered no interest. My team and I had tried everything. Then, one day, I asked a question that had come to me while working out the day before.

"What was life like here before the Soviets came?"

When I asked the most senior elder this, his eyes widened. He had not seen that question coming. Then they misted over. His lip trembled, and he began to speak. Slowly at first, but then in a torrent. His voice filled the room as he described what his village was like before decades of war and famine had plagued his people into a state of inescapable shock. The Russians, a civil war, the Taliban, and now NATO soldiers.

He smiled. He talked about Friday picnics on the lawn of the mosque. Music was in the air. Children would play. Stories were told. No one was blown up on the way home. "Better days," he said, his voice trailing off.

Then I asked, "What would it take to get back to those better days?" After that, we talked into the wee hours of the night. He and the other elders shared insights into what mattered to them and the obstacles that needed to be overcome.

This village became one of the most participatory communities we worked with in the war.

There is another universal lesson for storytelling that you can take from these rough places: *It's not always the stories we tell that change hearts and minds...It's the stories we ask to hear.*

If you want your intention to be pure discovery, then thoughtful, open-ended questions allow the other party to respond in narratives we immediately understand and remember. Their answers give us insights into the pain and goals of the people we aim to serve. When they respond with their own story, the emotional temperature is lowered, context is provided, and we can see the images in their heads. A decisive point.

When trust is low and the stakes are high, the deepest form of narrative competence is often contained in the stories we *ask* to hear. Said differently, if you want a beautiful answer, ask a beautiful question.[22]

You'll soon learn about the struggles of others, which will make them receptive to hearing about your own struggles. And as we will see in the next chapter, nothing brings human beings together like struggle.

CHAPTER 8

Struggle
or, Be Generous with Your Scars

The cave you fear to enter holds the treasure you seek.

—Joseph Campbell

Be Generous with Your Scars

The Merriam-Webster dictionary defines "scar" as "a mark remaining (as on the skin) after injured tissue has healed."

I have a slightly different definition: "an emotionally charged and often secret mark buried in the soul, earned through trauma and struggle, that has the potential to form connective tissue with the outside world." Or, if brevity is your thing: "a hidden mark borne of struggle."

Survivor's guilt is a big part of my story. Why am I still here when so many of my sisters and brothers from the war are not?

Some of these people died doing things I had asked them to do. Others died after the war by their own hands. These are people I should have checked in on more but didn't. How could I move past this?

By owning my guilt.

I regularly tell audiences that storytelling is being generous with your scars. On the surface, this means just telling your story, even if doing so is scary or embarrassing. But deeper down, it means sharing the root struggle that has actively scarred you.

Being generous with scars doesn't happen easily. We usually want to hide the kind of scars I'm talking about. Being generous with them almost always means getting below the waterline in a tough way. That was how it had to go down with me.

You probably won't be surprised to learn that Bo Eason helped me with this. He had me work with an amazing story coach named Jean-Louis Rodrigue, who teaches the physicality of storytelling and pushed me toward generosity with my scars. In our first day of working together, Jean-Louis could tell my body was racked with tension. It all started when he said, "Tell me more about your backstory, Scott."

"What, from childhood?"

"No. About the friends you've lost. I'd like to learn their names."

"What are you talking about?" I asked. I immediately got defensive It felt like he was picking at some private thing within me.

Picking at my scar.

"I want you to see them and connect with them as you speak their names," Jean-Louis encouraged. "If you see them, we'll see them."

"I don't think I can do that," I said, my voice cracking.

"These guys are part of your story, Scott. Invite them to be with you," Jean-Louis said with a kind smile.

I was suddenly panicked. But he stood there, resolute, holding space for me. I took a breath. Then I started to say the names of the friends I'd lost. For most of them, it was the first time I'd uttered their names since attending their funerals. I had a really hard time saying the names of one specific person who had died following my orders. I started to cry, and this quickly became sobbing. The ugly, snotty kind. I couldn't breathe.

After a little while, the sobs subsided. I wiped my nose and tears. Jean-Louis walked over and gave me a hug. "Okay, good," he said softly. "Now you're ready to tell your story. And theirs."

That was the moment I began to let go of my guilt and shame. That was the moment I began to integrate their stories into mine. That was the moment I started to realize my own power again. That was when I began to connect with the narrative of my own life.

It was, without question, a pivotal moment.

To this day, I say the names of at least five of my fallen buddies every time I tell a story. Pedro Munoz. Charlie Robinson.

Vic Cervantes. Chris Piper. Cliff Patterson. Eighteen more. All these years later, it's a way to keep their memory alive. And remembering them has helped keep me alive.

Speaking of that, it took me four years to tell Monty what happened in the closet that day. It was 2019. We were rapidly approaching a trip to Santa Barbara so I could deliver a TED Talk, a follow-up to one I'd delivered on Rooftop Leadership. We'd been in Buffalo or Youngstown just before, I can't remember which—mainly because I'd just lost another veteran friend to suicide.

I realized I couldn't give the talk I'd planned. I needed to talk about what had happened in that closet when I pushed the cold muzzle of my .45 into my skin.

That night in our hotel, I said, "Babe, I can't do my TED Talk. I need to change it." With the talk just a few weeks away, Monty looked at me like I was crazy. "I want it to be about the generosity of scars," I said. "I want it to be about mental health and veteran suicide."

"Okay, baby," she said reassuringly. "You want to share how the suicides of your friends have impacted you?"

"Yeah. But there's more." I swallowed hard. "We need to talk."

That was when I told her about that afternoon in 2015, and how close I had come to killing myself. If I was going to talk about this with a roomful of strangers, I had to tell her first. She wasn't particularly surprised. She knew I'd been in a terrible place, a place we didn't talk about. Then I told my boys. God, that was hard. It still is. A few weeks later, with knees trembling, I stood in the red circle and shared it with the world.

Afterward, it was obvious that I was in a better place. I'd brought so many of my storytelling skills to bear: narrative competence; it's not about you; narrative transportation; pivotal moments; storytelling 301. I used my body and the tone of my voice and my words. I took the audience on one of my Hero's Journeys. It was cathartic.

So many people came up to me after the talk—veteran and civilian—to say they had stood in their own version of that closet, thinking they were all alone. The talk, as difficult as it was, now has over a million views on YouTube.*

That was the day I fully understood that when we are generous with our scars, new opportunities to serve others arrive.

Why? Because we all struggle. It's universal. Repurposing our struggle so that others can find hope is the ultimate form of generosity. It is the rocket fuel for leading through the Churn.

A Biological Necessity

We are a community of sufferers.[23]

---

*If you'd like to check out my TED Talk "The Generosity of Scars," you can find it here: https://youtu.be/_szAosvdWdM.

As the author Daniel Coyle explains in his book *The Little Book of Talent*, struggle occurs when the brain is forced to build new neural pathways to overcome a challenge. Struggle isn't something that happens to a few of us. It's a biological necessity for all of us.[24]

No one is exempt.

We all struggle.

Yet when I look around our tip-of-the iceberg world, I see very little recognition of struggle. It's almost like it's been removed from our language.

Consider some imaginary CEO who never acknowledges her own shortcomings. All she talks about is "Five ways to be great like me." There's no humility, no sense of how she got to where she is. It's almost like she came into the world an executive. Which we all know isn't true. So, what do we do? We check out. The phones come out and we drift away.

People are starved for leaders who integrate struggle into their presentations, into their *stories*. When a CEO admits to her career (and life) struggles and talks about them, a junior associate says to themselves, *Wow she's been through a lot, just like me. Maybe I can do this too.*

Leaders who integrate struggle into their personal and organizational visions are immediately relatable. They accelerate trust. They set the emotional temperature just right, so that the people they serve are primed to listen.

They struggle. You struggle. We struggle.

It's a biological necessity.

Flowers Grow out of Rocky Ground

This shit isn't easy. I get it. I want to sprint out of the room before most of my keynotes even begin. I want to throw up before most performances of *Last Out*. Why go through the pain of being generous with your scars? It's so uncomfortable. It's so *personal*.

Well, you go through it because it's worth it. For you, sure—but more importantly, for the people you serve.

Time and again, I've watched people who have been through terrible tragedies and trauma repurpose their struggles into stories that serve others. A mother who lost her husband and young daughter in a freak plane accident at the beach who is now an organ donor advocate. A widow who lost her firefighter husband to a sudden stroke who now does fundraising for nonprofits. A CIA paramilitary officer who shares his near suicide to help other veterans overcome mental health issues.

These examples are truly traumatic, but struggle (and trauma) comes in all shapes and sizes. No one has to die or get maimed for your struggles to be relevant to others. If you just catalog your more "mundane" struggles and share those, it will give people hope. You're still here. You made it. Maybe I can make it too.

One of the most important figures in Operation Pineapple Express was a State Department official named JP who was in Kabul as it fell. When it was all over, I was in a dark place. I was pissed at the US military and the civilian leadership, and I felt horribly guilty about the people we couldn't get out. I felt viscerally guilty about a group of orphan girls we desperately tried to save but who were ultimately killed by an ISIS-K suicide bomber at Abbey Gate. How did it all go so wrong? *Why* did it all go so wrong?

JP shared my frustrations, but he was more optimistic. He had been there, after all, and I'd been holed up in my man cave in Tampa staring at screens twenty hours a day and barely eating. He had access to more information—not the kind you get from reports or briefings, but the kind you get with your eyes and ears, with your smell, with your touch.

"Flowers grow out of rocky ground, Scott," he said to me one day as he stood to depart from our only in-person meeting. "In the same hectic Kabul Airport that saw immense suffering and death, some young couples fell in love. A baby was born. And some people got out."

The fact is, we never know how our stories of struggle will help light the path for others and enable them to find meaning in their own journey.

But know this: There is someone sitting out there who needs to hear about the flowers you've found, because all around them in their moment of pain is a bunch of rocks.

Yeah, it's hard work. But it's worth it.

No Struggle, No Story

Many leaders actively avoid revealing any element of struggle in their personal lives. "I don't want people to see me as weak," they'll protest. The soft skill myth strikes again. As we know by now, it's bullshit.

If you want to be relevant to people caught in the Churn, you must tell them a real and meaningful story. And if you want that, you'll have to deal with your struggles.

If there's no struggle, there's no story.

Let's go back to our working definition of story, with some added emphasis: a detailed, character-based narration of *a character's struggles* to overcome obstacles and reach an important goal.[25]

We are meaning-seeking creatures, and we can't experience the satisfaction of resolution if there is nothing to resolve. If Rocky Balboa knocked out Apollo Creed in the first round, you'd get up and walk out of the movie. And Sylvester Stallone's fellow filmmakers would be out a few Oscars.

But it goes beyond this. Not only is struggle an essential element of storytelling, but in our low-trust world, if you leave struggle out of your narrative then your audience will turn on you. Your lack of struggle translates directly to lack of authenticity. This will cause some people to actively oppose the goals you're trying to achieve. They become a *narrative insurgent* to the idea or message you are trying to get across. And it's happening everywhere you look.*

The exhausted majority you're trying to reach craves leaders whose stories are built on the shoulders of struggle. It bridges the gaps of race, religion, and politics. It accelerates trust and makes you immediately relatable. It shows that you are not, in fact, weak. It shows that you're the exact opposite.

Universal Singulars

When we were conducting Village Stability Operations in Afghanistan, I did a lot of storytelling with rural farmers. Our mission was to get them to allow us to live in their village and to convince them to fight alongside us on the rooftops against the Taliban. It was a gargantuan ask for us to make after ten years of explosive targeting operations in these same communities, and us living on built-up firebases far removed from these villagers.

As you might imagine, there was immediate skepticism and reluctance. I knew that I needed to make a human connection

---

*Dr. Kendall Haven shared this groundbreaking discovery with me in a 2020 interview. I believe it's a game changer for leaders to know that if they omit struggle from the stories they tell, their audience will likely turn on them.

before anything else. The villagers needed to see me as Scott, not as some faceless soldier who would rotate home in another six months.

So I focused on a universal singular: farming.

Low-tech farming, to be more exact.

Ninety-five percent of Afghanistan is agrarian. Farming there is universal. And very primitive.

I told stories about tobacco farming as a kid. This type of farming is also primitive. Even in the twenty-first century, it's done almost entirely by hand. My dad always said, "Growing tobacco is the only form of farming where you slowly starve to death as you do it." The Afghan elders, who relied on subsistence farming after years of drought, loved that quote. They would laugh out loud. They'd never met my dad. They'd never seen a tobacco farm. But they instinctively connected with the universal singular of low-tech farming in hard times.

More accurately, they connected with the universal singular of struggle *within the context of farming.* There are other universal singulars you can leverage. Things below the waterline that bind us: Faith, family, food, and dreams are just a few. It takes some prep work, but the more you get to know your audience, the more you can select universal singulars that resonate with them (and you) when it comes time to tell your story.

By doing some prep work before engaging with the villagers, I was able to leverage the struggles of farming. I could share my pain around this challenging but rewarding way of life.

This made me more relatable, which enabled me to ask more questions about their own struggles, their own pain.

We didn't talk about the Taliban. Or elections. Or village stability.

We talked about farming. And we kept passing these stories back and forth until something clicked between us. The click of rapport, of human connection. Once this was established, I probed a little deeper, and then a little deeper still, always careful about the pace the village elders were comfortable with. Eventually we got to other subjects, and after a long time they joined us on the rooftops.

Look around. Who do you serve? What's their pain? Do you know it? Do they know yours? What are their goals? What are the universal singulars that you can use to build stories and questions? What struggles can you share to bridge gaps, build trust, and bring people together?

People Choose the Storyteller First

Narrative transportation—using the sights, smells, and physical settings of a place to make it feel real for the listener—is critical to good storytelling.

There's a method to narrative transportation, which I wrote about in the previous section. But it doesn't just have to do with the senses. It also—and primarily—has to do with struggle.

People locate themselves first and foremost in your narrated struggle. When you talk about struggle successfully and authentically, the body armor falls away and people open up. This moment is decisive. It's the moment people choose you, the storyteller.

That's right. People choose you long before they choose your message. We are social creatures living in low-trust times, and we are not going to buy into an idea before we connect to the human who delivers it. If people do buy in before connecting with the storyteller, it will be a shallow, transactional choice. As soon as any pressure is applied to them, they'll bounce. This is one big reason so many institutional leaders lose people—they forget that they should be revealing their scars before unveiling their ideas.

When you're trying to move people to action or a new way of thinking, you want them to choose you first, then your message. This is precisely why it's so critical to build your personal and organizational narratives on the sturdy shoulders of struggle.

The Personal Is Universal

We now know that struggle is a universal singular that binds us together, and that talking about your struggles makes you more relatable as a storyteller.

But what kind of struggle? What is the best struggle to convey when you're trying to move people to action, whether that's to get up on the rooftop and fight with you, navigate a merger, or lead your nonprofit through a crisis?

The personal kind.

According to psychologist Carl R. Rogers, "What's most personal is most universal."

This idea is anathema to our mechanistic, mass-technology world. We are conditioned not to make anything personal—unless it's an insult.

But our human nature, built upon tens of thousands of years of storytelling, declares emphatically that if it's personal to you, then it will be universally relevant to your audience. If it matters to you, it will matter to them.

Revealing and conveying our personal struggles isn't easy to do in our era of Churn. As soon as we go there, self-doubt kicks in and we start rationalizing. We think, *No one wants to hear what I have to say. Why should the things that are important to me be important to anyone else? Who am I to share this?* If you do decide to share them, then you start to worry. *Am I putting myself at risk? What will people think? What is this going to cost me?*

It will cost you nothing. If you do it authentically—hell, you don't even have to do it well, you just have to be real about it—then they will think you're awesome. And you're damn right you're putting yourself at risk. That's the name of the game.

Making it personal is the most effective way to separate yourself from the divisionists and establish yourself as trustworthy. From here you can shake the masses from their trance state, as well as reach their machine-infatuated brains and show them how to reclaim their right-hemisphere birthright as human beings.

Making it personal takes some homework. As with universal singulars, you'll have to do some research so you can understand the people you serve, their pain, their goals, and the pictures in their heads. Once you're reasonably confident of these, you are free to generously share stories about the things that are personal to you in that same context. And once you do, you'll find yourself in a position of relevance that is unmatched.

This is a mode of work that requires moral courage that many can't summon. But you must.

Nowadays, we need to move large numbers of people through rough times. We must make it personal in order to make it universal.

Don't Just Be Vulnerable, Be Relatable

Leveraging the "what's personal is universal" principle of scar generosity requires a commitment to being vulnerable. The willingness—some would say the need—to be vulnerable pops up in some unexpected places. Author Daniel Coyle writes about Navy SEAL commanders who "signal vulnerability" in combat to more effectively achieve their team's objectives. This surprises many people who have false perceptions of combat leaders that have been spread around by Hollywood and paperback thrillers.

I've seen the power of vulnerability in combat myself, and more times than I can count. The leaders I found to be most authentic and worthy of personal sacrifice were those who were willing to admit when they had gaps in knowledge or needed advice.

In fact, the ability to be vulnerable in any high-stakes situation is extremely valuable. Yet so many in our transactional world still have a lot of problems with the "V" word. These people feel they're putting themselves at risk; they worry that they're sticking out their jugular in a cutthroat world. I get it.

So try a little adjustment. Don't just be "vulnerable." Be "relatable." We're social creatures and as such, we're predisposed to relate to one another.

Ask yourself, "Am I being relatable to my teenager right now? Does my audience relate to the story I'm telling about the cause I support? Am I asking thoughtful, open-ended questions that will allow her to respond with stories that I can relate to?"

When you honestly and openly pursue relatability, vulnerability will show up naturally, almost as a by-product. If it gives you the shakes, you won't have to wrestle with the "V" word at all.

The Two Best Scar Stories

I've taught narrative competence to men, women, and kids who've been through some of the most terrible experiences imaginable. Suicide. Combat loss. Combat injury. Rape. Divorce.

Scars.

I've trained a young man named Billy whose two childhood strokes were so severe that he lost 70 percent of his cerebellum. He went on to deliver a TED Talk that received the only standing ovation of the day and has inspired thousands online.

I've taught a young teenager to share her story of losing her military dad to suicide. She's told her story in one-on-one crisis moments and in support groups where children of suicide victims struggle with acute levels of isolation and depression.

Tough stuff.

But here's the good news. It makes no difference what your background is, whether or not you have a title, or how old you are. If you're human, the generosity of scars is available to you. All you need is the will and courage to employ it in the service of others.

There is one mandatory rule, however—the effort requires all of you. Otherwise, it's just a speech or a pitch. And we already have too many of those.

There are two great stories to share through the generosity of scars.

The second-best scar story is the story you don't want to tell others.

The best scar story is the story you don't want to tell yourself.

Because *that* story is the *exact* story someone else needs to hear to save them from their own demons. When I shared my mental health challenges and suicidal ideation on that TED stage, I was embarrassed and mortified. I didn't want to talk about it. I didn't want to tell this story to myself or anyone else. But I did. And—no joke—I know it has saved lives.

It's one of my very best scar stories.

What's Your Scar Story?

So how about it? What's your scar story? What are the moments of struggle you can share through purposeful storytelling in the service of others?

Figuring this out can be daunting, but the initial process is quite simple.

There's a modified version of the Hero's Journey that you can use to start discovering and crafting your scar story right now.

Go someplace quiet. Someplace where you feel grounded. Maybe somewhere sacred to you. Take a pen and a pad of paper. Don't use a computer, phone, or tablet. Otherwise, you're not giving your right brain its due and you're activating our modern tendency to imitate our machines. Then, for ten minutes, write your scar story. Don't edit. Don't read. Just write.

Start by pinpointing a pivotal moment that changed the trajectory of your life. In a few minutes you're going to describe it, but not so fast. First, describe the ordinary world just before that moment occurred. Just a few sentences of what life looked like before that ball of chaos dropped into your life. Then describe the pivotal moment. What did the room look like when you got the news? What sounds could you hear? Was there a bird outside? A garbage truck? Was your baby crying? Could you smell anything? What were you wearing? After you heard the news, what happened in your body? How did you physically feel? When you eventually tell your story, these details will be indispensable. They will help transport your listener to your world. You'll have them hooked.

Then, tell them about that ball of chaos.

As you start to recover, take them on your journey. Where did you go, what did you do? Move into the "belly of the whale" part of the story. Describe the struggles you faced. What were the internal conflicts? What were the external obstacles? What was the risk of failure? What were the consequences if you failed? What were the sensory memories you have about the obstacles? Remember, what's personal is universal. You'll be tempted to skim over some of this stuff. Don't. Embrace the suck for the moment. Struggle is where people choose you.

Move on. Did a guide show up to help you? Describe her. How did she help you? It could be something as simple as Jean-Louis Rodrigue helping me say the names of the guys I lost in combat. Don't skip over the guide—this is another universal singular for storytelling that accelerates connection. We each have our own Obi-Wan Kenobi who guides us through the storm.

And then, resolution. What happened on the other side of the struggle? Did you meet your goal? Did you fail? If you did, that's okay. People fail constantly. Talk about how that felt, about the pain that engendered. How did you change because of your struggle? What did you learn about yourself? About the world? About others? About love? About hate? About forgiveness? Who did you help? Did you hurt anyone? How has everything panned out?

Have any of these resolutions sent you on additional journeys? Because they often do...

That's it. Those are the building blocks of a powerful scar story. It's up to you to choose how weighty your pivotal moment will be. Maybe it's when you learned your wife had cancer. But maybe it's when you found out you were having a boy when you were 100 percent certain you were having a girl. Maybe it's when you found an old toy or drawing from your childhood when you were cleaning out your dad's attic. Maybe it was when you almost killed yourself in your closet. Maybe it was when you said goodbye to your teenage daughter this morning before school but made sure to give her a real hug first. She looked at you funny, and then left. She came home, nothing terrible happened—but that hug still felt heavy. It still felt like a little win, all on its own. Why? I don't know.

Tell us.

Active Trauma and Deep Grief

As a caution: Some stories take time to put into the world. Don't share something that's not resolved within you yet or is white hot in your brain. That's not good for you or the people you serve. A story can't serve others until there is resolution. But that's not a pass to ignore its narrative power. Work it through in counseling or therapy. Then dare to share that story in the service of others. It's likely to become one of the most powerful stories in your narrative arsenal.

But What If I Fall Apart?

Good.

When you fall apart, all it means is that it matters. And if it matters to you, it can and will matter to others when you tell them about it. (To be clear, I'm not talking about reliving trauma in front of an audience, but rather an appropriate emotional response to the telling of your story…the things that move you inside.)

As you're falling apart—if you can manage to speak—you'll feel the urge to say two insane words to your audience.

"I'm sorry."

Why is this? Why do we apologize for expressing emotions that demonstrate our humanity to fellow humans? We all go through this shit. We all fall apart. I don't care how tough you are. In the course of our lives—funerals, weddings, talks with our kids, all-hands meetings, recognition of teammates—when emotions are involved, we're all headed to the same place: You're going to fall apart. More than once. Take a breath and try to move through it. For some reason, we've been subconsciously conditioned to panic and apologize like this. It needs to stop.

Here's the thing. If you share your story in the service of your listener, you'll be just fine. Even if you get emotional, so long as it's within the context of serving your audience, then it will be received as nothing less than deep generosity. All this will do is draw you closer together.

Now, you don't want to completely fall apart and lose emotional control in front of your audience. If at any point during a TED Talk or a performance of *Last Out* I were to explore topics I'd repressed for years for the first time onstage and sob like a child as I had in front of Jean-Louis, then the people watching would get worried about me and they'd cease to hear my message. Someone might come onstage to check on me. I hope they would. If I was in the audience and the speaker fell apart like that, I'd probably get up there to check on her.

But this doesn't mean you should repress your emotions. Far from it. Tears, anger, and laughter are beautiful within the natural context of a story. It's like plugging into a wall socket and allowing the emotional energy to move through you. Don't cheat yourself or your audience out of that experience.

Like a lot of other things in this book, navigating your emotions while sharing stories of struggle takes some practice. But once you get the hang of it, it's not difficult. Do the emotional work as a part of storytelling preparation, and your emotions will join your storytelling in beautiful and appropriate ways.

Since we've been conditioned to equate emotion to falling apart, we often hold our breath when we start to get emotional. This sends a primal signal to the brain that there's an emergency. Your emotional temperature elevates into a sympathetic state, and suddenly you can look like you don't trust yourself. Think stage fright, but with the pre-sob belly shakes, weak knees, and the hair on your nape standing on end. You can feel that, right? Doesn't feel great.

If this happens, just breathe. If you feel emotion coming on, that's fine. Just let go into your body with a big exhale.

Keep breathing. Feel your feet on the floor. Allow the emotion to blow in and out like the wind.

It will come in waves and pass within ninety seconds.

And if you want to move through it faster—or if you must

because you're onstage—simply take a step or two to the left or right, and it will dissipate within twenty to twenty-five seconds.

Times are hard. People are hurting. Leaders are cold and transactional. If you show up with emotional access that is authentic and available, and you genuinely serve your audience, they will relate to you even more, and the reciprocity will grow like a flower in rocky ground.

The Rise of the Exhausted Majority

We Need No Titles, We Need No Permission

It wasn't Operation Pineapple Express that made me realize we can get big shit done when nobody is coming. That realization came afterward.

Following a successful sixteen-city tour in 2019, *Last Out* was released as a movie on Amazon Prime on Veterans Day 2021, fewer than three months after the Taliban took Kabul. Thousands of veterans, reeling from the moral injury of Afghanistan's collapse and our rushed exit, watched the film and thanked us for validating their work and sacrifice. Military spouses and children beamed with pride, saying they saw their lives reflected in the film. As the film gathered steam, we built an online following called "Friends of Last Out" that spans the globe. Maybe the thing I'm most proud of is that we produced a film to reach our veteran community when the pandemic shut down our tour. From stage and screen, our story was informative, validating, and healing—and it was helping people across the country.

One day, John Ondrasik, a dear friend and recording artist, called. He'd been helping Afghan refugees in his own way, and he'd recently seen the film. "Scott," he said, "I think you need to get *Last Out* in front of Gary Sinise," the actor and veterans' advocate.

I agreed. I'd been trying—and failing—to get *Last Out* to him for some time. His play about Vietnam vets, *Tracers*, had been hugely influential for me.

"He's a little busy, don't you think?" I asked John.

"We're all busy. So what? He's a good friend. I'll give him a call. He needs to see this."

"Okay," I said, but I was skeptical.

Two days later, I got a text from Gary. "Scott, can you talk?"

My heart pounded. I called him immediately. We spoke for two hours, like we were old friends. I walked up and down my driveway, phone pressed to my ear, the whole time.

We talked about *Forrest Gump* and his role as Lieutenant Dan. We talked about his play, and mine. "*Tracers* helped heal the moral injury of Vietnam," I said at one point. "A lot of our veteran community is hurting from the deep moral injury from the way we left Afghanistan. I believe this is a modern-day

Tracers and that more people should see it." I told him we'd made it all from the bottom up, and that we were out of resources.

He said he wanted to help. By the summer of 2022, we'd assembled a new production of *Last Out*, thanks to the Gary Sinise Foundation. We kicked off a national tour in January 2023, starting at the same theater that had premiered *Tracers* in 1980—the iconic Steppenwolf Theatre in Chicago. We sold out every show. Standing ovations erupted after each performance, followed by hard-hitting talk-backs between the cast and the audience.

As we resumed touring, we made sure that every production had certified counselors right in the audience. Since 2019, these counselors have conducted hundreds of post-traumatic stress interventions during and after the show. We were meeting people where they were and helping them on the spot.

When I first told people I was going to use storytelling in a play to inform Americans about the cost of war while simultaneously helping veterans and their families let go of the pain of war, people thought I was crazy. Yet within just five years of us dreaming up the project, the scar story that should never have gotten off the ground had grown into a multimillion-dollar nonprofit project, sponsored by Gary Sinise, educating civilians and helping thousands of veterans and their families heal from the trauma of war.

But it wasn't the money we raised, or the miles we traveled, or the accolades we received that told me *Last Out* was working. It was the people we touched. People like Corey Briest, a veteran with the Army National Guard.

Corey had come to a performance in Vermillion, South Dakota, with his wife, kids, and father. He was in the front row in his wheelchair. A roadside bomb in Iraq had badly injured Corey in 2005. He was partially paralyzed, had lost most of his eyesight, and suffered from a traumatic brain injury that impaired many of his day-to-day functions, including speech.

The lights went down, the play began. In one scene, Master Sergeant Danny Patton, the lead character, tells his wife, Lynn, about the rubber silly band their son, Caiden, had given him at breakfast that morning. Danny was about to redeploy to Afghanistan, and Caiden wanted to do something for his dad. "It's a magic silly band, Daddy. Don't take it off. It'll keep you safe." Danny promised it would never leave his wrist. Lynn, a superstitious woman determined not to lose her husband, made him promise again. "Don't you ever take it off!"

As this scene played out, I could hear moaning coming from the front row. I knew Corey was there—we'd met earlier that evening. It's difficult to see audience members when you're in the lights, but I could just make Corey out, rocking back and forth in his wheelchair. It comforted me.

We kept going. The show went on.

Afterward, Corey's dad pushed him up to me in the theater's lobby where the cast gathered to meet audience members. I thanked them both for coming and asked them what they thought.

"We loved it," Corey's dad said. "Do you know what his favorite part was?"

"The silly band scene?" I asked.

"That's right," his dad said. When I asked why, he pointed to Corey's arm. "Do you see that white ring of skin on Corey's wrist?" I bent over and looked. There was a stark white ring contrasting with his darker skin. I took a knee beside him and nodded to his dad. "His daughter's silly band was right there when the bomb went off. It was seared to his skin." Corey's father choked back tears. "He never took his off, either."

I had a hard time not falling over on the spot. Tears suddenly streamed down my cheeks. Corey started crying too. These were those good tears, the ones that make you feel cracked open while they tell you your feelings are all right.

This was not my first experience with "life imitating art," but it was by far the most meaningful. Corey had located himself in our story, had found meaning out of a simple green silly band. Right in front of me was the power of so many things I've tried to unpack in this book—narrative competence, the physical act of storytelling, narrative transportation, pivotal moments, universal singulars, suffering, connection, trust, reciprocity, authenticity, the fact that it's not about you at all but about the story—all of these came together for a minute or two in the middle of a two-hour play. The work we'd done, the story we had told, helped Corey validate his suffering and the journey he was still taking. My hope is that it also gave him a new perspective on the war we all fought, together.

That night, I showed Corey my metaphorical scar, and he showed me the one he carried with him everywhere on his wrist. The one he could not—and would not—take off.

How do you place a value on moments like these? You don't. How do you measure the merit of this type of connection? You can't. What could be better for our ancient souls than this kind of deep work? If there is something better, I'm not aware of it.

By the rules of our transactional, modern society, this never should have happened. I had no acting experience. I'd never written a play.

So what? I did it, lots of people helped, and here we are.

We need no titles to do this kind of work. We need no permission. We just need the will, the courage, and the skill of human connection to make it happen.

To the Upswing!

Do you believe that abundance is an entitlement? Something we deserve as a species?

I don't.

Don't get me wrong, I love living in a society of abundance. But I believe it must be earned and protected through responsible leadership that eclipses the amateurish, self-centered nature of divisionism and the corresponding shadow tribalism we see so much of today. I believe we must be stewards of abundance.

Civil society doesn't lend itself to this kind of stewardship if too many of us are stuck in the Churn of our left-brain trance state. It's difficult to protect our common resources if we're disconnected, distracted, disengaged, and full of distrust. We look around these days and see contempt between people, moral superiority, even violence. These are encouraged by the Churn. It doesn't have to be this way. That's on us.

To get past this—or more precisely, over it—we need to build bridges. To each other and over the river of distrust that courses between us. The social scientists Jonathan Haidt and Robert Putnam speak of American society as one that, despite our differences, offers a unique opportunity for community and fulfillment if we can just manage to bridge our way to trust.

And here's the thing: We've been here before, so don't let the naysayers convince you all is hopeless. It isn't. They're just being divisionist. They're just lining their pockets.

Putnam describes an America in the early 1900s that was in a severe social capital downswing. A massive wealth gap divided people into haves and have-nots. Lots of political and cultural groups viewed their opponents as full-on enemies. Population was surging in urban areas and stagnating or declining across the rural countryside. Deeply polarized politicians and pundits opined that America was in her final days.

Sound familiar?

Nevertheless, things were happening below the surface Churn in 1900. Things were getting MESSSy. Take Dr. Bob and Bill W., a couple of drunks from Akron, Ohio. They desperately wanted to get sober, but nobody was coming to save them. So they held a meeting, just the two of them. They talked about drinking, and not drinking, and wanting to drink, and not wanting to drink, and family, and faith, and everything. They told stories of struggle about themselves. They connected. They were there for each other. The word spread. More people came to their meetings, and then more. They called their group Alcoholics Anonymous. Since then, millions upon millions of alcoholics and addicts from all around the world have found sobriety and recovery because of AA, including this humble author.

But that's not all. In 1901, Mary Harriman started a new volunteer organization in New York City devoted to helping poor women—she called it the Junior League, and it is still alive and well. In 1909, W. E. B. Du Bois joined with other prominent civil rights activists to form the National Association for the Advancement of Colored People, an organization devoted to combating racism, segregation, and violence against African Americans. It is as relevant today as it was over a hundred years ago. In 1919, Paul Harris convened a meeting with three business colleagues in Chicago to address local community issues. They called themselves the Rotary Club, which is now an international organization with 1.4 million members and over 6,400 chapters. That same year, a bottom-up, grass-roots movement that began in earnest in 1848 in Seneca Falls, New York, saw its long-sought goals achieved when Congress passed the Nineteenth Amendment, granting women full voting rights across the United States.

In fact, the first seventy or so years of the twentieth century reads like a who's who of American civil and social organizations: the American Civil Liberties Union; the Boy Scouts; the Girl Scouts; the American Red Cross; the American Heart Association; the National Audubon Society; Veterans of Foreign Wars; the League of Women Voters; Amnesty International; the American Association for Retired Persons; the Nature Conservancy; Meals on Wheels; the Sierra Club; and on and on. All of these and more came into being in a flurry of civic activity between roughly 1900 and 1970.

And then, around the time Nixon resigned after Watergate, things started falling apart again. Our current downswing doesn't look much different from Putnam's description of America in the early 1900s: We're divided, we're angry, the rich are getting richer, and the rest of us are treading water or backsliding.

But Putnam believes we are on the cusp of another grassroots upswing. So do I.

So, what are we going to do about it?

We're going to get to work from the bottom up. We're going to operationalize our own upswing. Your operation can be as small as leading your town council, or it can be as big as tackling homelessness. You can take on fentanyl, or you can take on literacy challenges with the students you teach. You can advocate for veterans, or you can advocate for your family. You can create a product line that makes our lives better, or healthier. You can lead at-risk kids on multiday camping trips, or you can lead coworkers to show more corporate responsibility. Whatever you do, I believe the time is now for good old-fashioned bottom-up leadership in America. If we can redefine our purpose, if we can use our struggles to come together, if we can share meaningful stories and listen to them, if we can embrace our MESSSy natures, then we can feed our very starved right brain, get back outside, and make more connections. We can be stewards of the abundance we are all so fortunate to share.

To the upswing!

Bottom-Up Leads to Top-Down

But what about the institutional leaders in politics, media, corporate America, and other critical organizations who are dividing us? We're just going to let them slide?

No, we're not. Bottom-up leadership is critical, but we can't truly thrive without the top-down leadership of institutions that are also necessary repositories of civil society. We need them. But what about the divisionists who have lost our trust and are driving us off the cliff? We need to vote them out. We need to replace them with leaders from the Rooftop.

I know that's not always possible, not yet. Where it isn't, our "leaders" need to be inspired, influenced, or even shamed into doing what's right by our bottom-up efforts to serve the exhausted majority instead of serving themselves. We need to shine bright sunlight on their bad behavior with the collective actions of mobilized citizens doing good work from the grass roots. Hell, even institutional leaders can adopt a Rooftop approach.

Bottom-up actions can and do bring pressure for top-down reform. During the upswing that started around 1900, Teddy Roosevelt listened to the grassroots movements all around and enacted a series of top-down, nation-changing reforms. As America's twenty-sixth president, he broke up monopolies, established early labor rights, signed laws safeguarding food and medicine, regulated the railroads, and birthed the National Park System.

These kinds of things can happen again. Bottom-up initiatives can show top-down leaders how to lead. It's not just the way it *can* work in America, it's the way it has *always* worked. Our businesses can thrive. Our economy can brim with hope and possibility. We are free to dream. We can share in our abundance and still be individuals. Eventually, our leaders will get the memo:

True leadership is more contagious than fear.

The Empowered Majority

You might be asking, "What's the point? No matter how hard I work at human connection and building communities of practice around wicked problems, the Churn has already engulfed the country."

Not so fast. The divisionists want you to believe that they hold the most ground, and that you should give up.

But the divisionists are wrong, and you cannot give up.

According to an in-depth, yearlong study of eight thousand Americans by the nonprofit More in Common on the issue of division in America, there are seven ideological tribes in the United States. Only 33 percent of these tribes form the extreme left and the extreme right, which are in the wings of political opinion.[26]

These two extremes—which are incessantly amplified by divisionists in media and people in positions of power—are drowning out the other tribes that comprise two-thirds of Americans: the exhausted majority. This bears repeating: *two-thirds of Americans!* In a true democracy, two-thirds is a supermajority that cannot be overcome. And yet the exhausted majority feels as though it is being overcome all the time.

These Americans are not necessarily centrists. They don't just sit in the middle on relevant issues. In fact, the study shows that their range of thinking on a variety of contentious national issues are as diverse as their race, religion, and socioeconomic status. What makes them different from the squawking divisionist minority dominating the public square is that they share the following positions:

- They are fed up with the polarization plaguing American government and society.
- They are often forgotten in the public discourse, overlooked because their voices are seldom heard.
- They are flexible in their views, willing to endorse different policies according to the situation.
- They are not ideologically rigid.
- They believe we can stand together on common ground.

For now, the divisionists are wearing us down. They have the microphones. While these ideologues argue and attack one another, veterans, small business owners, and community leaders are so depleted from the never-ending spew of modern politics that they simply check out altogether. This of course puts the microphones more firmly in the hands of these self-serving leaders, making it easier for them to continue to divide us.

What if we could change this? I believe we can.

The exhausted majority is right now becoming the empowered majority. There are thousands of movements underway to improve civil society, expand human connection, and deepen our social capital. Several of them have been identified in this book. These groups are modeling what leadership on tough problems needs to look like to our divisionist "leaders," while they continue to lecture us from the pulpit. As Jonathan Haidt says, "We cannot expect Congress and the tech companies to save us. We must change ourselves and our communities."

Nobody is coming to save us. That's okay by me.

I like those odds. I always have.

I'll run with this empowered majority—and you—all day long.

I'll see you on the Rooftop.

ACKNOWLEDGMENTS

To Randy Surles for all the years of bringing these stories into the sunlight. Thanks for your guidance and patience on helping me craft these stories and strategic lessons. It's been a great journey.

To combat infantryman turned editor, Chris Vetzel. Your mad copyediting skills made all the difference, pal. Keep going.

To Theo and Nils. You are the most amazing creatives and collaborators. This project wouldn't have been possible without your talent and patience.

To my agent, Howard Yoon, thanks for believing in this project. And in me.

To Alex Pappas and Center Street Publishing. You all are total pros and it's an honor to be part of your team.

To my Rooftop Leadership team of Wes, Stacey, and Amanda. Thanks for working so hard to make this book come to life every day.

To Emma Brannon. Thank you for your wonderful artwork in this book. Keep reaching, kiddo.

To my pal Steven Pressfield, thanks for always being a constant source of inspiration to me. Your definition of Resistance really helped me get my head around the Churn as an external foe.

To my dear friend Gary Sinise. Your support over the years means more than you'll ever know.

To my mentor and friend Bo Eason. Thanks for being there for me and pouring your hard-earned miles into me. I'll never forget it.

To all of the *Last Out* team members. You all made such an impact in the country with this story that's never been told in a voice never heard.

To Romy and Gaby Camargo, thank you for always leading from the front and showing the rest of us what leadership looks like.

To all of my brothers in Special Forces and the special ops community, to our veterans, and their families—thanks for teaching and mentoring me. And thank you for holding the line for the rest of us.

To my mom and dad, Rex and Anita Mann. Thanks for raising me right and never letting me forget where I come from.

To my boys, Cody, Cooper, and Brayden: You are the tracks I'm leaving.

Acknowledgments

To my wife, Monty, for being my ROCK—always.

To the EXHAUSTED MAJORITY. May you find your voice and a way to come together to drown out the divisionists, suppress the Churn, get big sh*t done, and lead us all into better days.

NOTES

1. Stephen Hawkins, Daniel Yudkin, Míriam Juan-Torres, and Tim Dixon, *Hidden: A Study of America's Polarized Landscape* (New York: More in Common, 2018), p. 5, https://hiddentribes.us.

2. Gloria Mark, *Attention Span: A Groundbreaking Way to Restore Balance, Happiness and Productivity* (Toronto: Hanover Square Press, 2023), p. 94.

3. Dr. Sahar Yousef, "The Science of Optimizing Productivity and Performance," Lecture to Emerging Leaders Conference, Washington, DC, March 18, 2024.

4. Jim Harter, "Disengagement Persists Among U.S. Employees," Gallup Workplace, April 25, 2022, www.gallup.com/workplace/391922/employee-engagement-slump-continues.aspx.

5. Lee Rainie, Scott Keeter, and Andrew Perrin, "Trust and Distrust in America," Pew Research Center, July 22, 2019, www.pewresearch.org/politics/2019/07/22/trust-and-distrust-in-america/.

6. Mark Weiner, *The Rule of the Clan: What an Ancient Form of Social Organization Reveals About the Future of Individual Freedom* (New York: Farrar, Straus & Giroux, 2013), p. 12.

7. Iain McGilchrist, *The Master and His Emissary: The Divided Brain and the Making of the Western World* (New Haven, CT, and London: Yale University Press, 2018), p. 38.

8. Laura Camón, "Like Humans, Animals Also Have Asymmetrical Brains," *El País*, December 7, 2022, https://english.elpais.com/science-tech/2022-12-07/like-humans-animals-also-have-asymmetrical-brains.html#.

9. Iain McGilchrist, "The Divided Brain," TED Talk, October 2011, www.ted.com/talks/iain_mcgilchrist_the_divided_brain.

10. Jared Diamond, "Why Study Traditional Societies?," *The Moon Magazine*, 2013, http://moonmagazine.org/jared-diamond-why-study-traditional-societies-2013-01-16/.

11. Jonathan Haidt, "Why the Past Ten Years of American Life Have Been Uniquely Stupid," *The Atlantic*, May 2022, www.theatlantic.com/magazine/archive /2022/05/social-media-democracy-trust-babel/629369/.

12. Sebastian Junger, *Tribe: On Homecoming and Belonging* (New York: Twelve, 2016), p. 125.

13. Matthew Lieberman, "The Social Brain and Its Superpowers," *Psychology Today*, October 8, 2013, www.psychologytoday.com/us/blog/social-brain-social -mind/201310/the-social-brain-and-its-superpowers.

14. McGilchrist, *The Master and His Emissary*, p. 397.

15. Ivan Tyrrell and Joe Griffin, *Human Givens: The New Approach to Emotional Health and Clear Thinking* (Chalvington, UK: Human Givens Publishing, 2015), pp. 6, 13.

16. Stuart Diamond, *Getting More: How You Can Negotiate to Succeed in Work and Life* (New York: Crown, 2010), p. 12.

17. Professor James Clawson, "Leadership as Managing Energy," *International Journal of Organizational Analysis* 16, no. 3 (November 2008):174–81, www.research gate.net/publication/270799777_Leadership_as_managing_energy.

18. Benjamin Hardy, *Personality Isn't Permanent: Break Free from Self-Limiting Beliefs and Rewrite Your Story* (New York: Portfolio, 2020), pp. 123–25.

19. Tyrrell and Griffin, *Human Givens*, p. 22.

20. Kendall Haven, *Story Proof: The Science Behind the Startling Power of Story* (Westport, UK: Libraries Unlimited, 2007), p. 79.

21. Chris Voss, *Never Split the Difference: Negotiate as If Your Life Depended on It* (New York: HarperCollins, 2016), p. 175.

22. Warren Berger, *The Book of Beautiful Questions: The Powerful Questions That Will Help You, Decide, Create, Connect, and Lead* (New York: Bloomsbury, 2018), p. 19.

23. Junger, *Tribe*, p. 53.

24. Daniel Coyle, *The Little Book of Talent: 52 Tips for Improving Your Skills* (New York: Bantam, 2012), p. 49.

25. Haven, *Story Proof*, p. 79.

26. Hawkins, Yudkin, Juan-Torres, and Dixon, *Hidden Tribes*, p. 6.

RESOURCES

Online Human Connection Courses

Now that you've read this book, if you find yourself fired up and ready to go deeper on the purpose and influence topics mentioned throughout this book, our online human connection courses are a great place to start. Especially if you are strapped for time and cash. If you enjoy learning through video courses and a self-paced tempo, we offer a virtual leadership platform where you will become better equipped to meet your goals through purpose, leadership, and human connection skills tested in some of the toughest places on earth. This monthly membership site is affordable and contains courses on clarity of purpose, narrative competence, negotiations, and much more that will help you get big sh*t done even when nobody is coming to save you. Go to www.scottmann.com to learn more or reach out to us here: info@scottmann.com.

Live Storytelling Workshop

The Churn is growing every day as the enemy to leadership. Distraction. Disengagement. Disconnection. Distrust. All these breed unprecedented fear and reluctance in your teams, clients, and community. In this increasingly transactional world, it's easy to feel like an imposter, unsure of yourself and this new landscape. When it comes to breaking through that glass ceiling, what got you here won't get you there.

What if you could OWN EVERY ROOM you walked into through relatability and relevance?

This two-day live immersive transformational experience will have you ready to champion the toughest issues you're facing today with the most powerful tool in your arsenal—your STORY! You've got the fire in your belly, now it's time to train with Scott and his amazing team of coaches. Go to www .scottmann.com to learn more or reach out to us here: info @scottmann.com.

Private Storytelling Workshop

Guiding your team through the process for getting big sh*t done by OWNING EVERY ROOM can be even more powerful when done within the comfort of your own team, in your own training space, or even off-site. There is something special about elite training around influence and impact with the people who stand at your shoulder every day. This two day private storytelling workshop features the same critical skills of purpose and influence as the public workshop. But it's also specifically geared to address the unique context, vision, and pain points of your organization. Your team will emerge with a shared language for appreciating the human operating system, strategically influencing through the Churn, telling the organization's story as well as their own, and leaving deep tracks of legacy and meaning in their life and business. Go to www .scottmann.com to learn more or reach out to us here: info @scottmann.com.

Executive Coaching Program

Do you want to lead a strategic movement? If after reading this book you feel something stirring deeply in your soul late at night when everyone else is sleeping, if you now hear a persistent voice telling you to do more, if you're feeling the call to do something that is about making a bigger impact in the world...and it scares the HELL out of you...you're in good company.

This program is for a handful of uniquely qualified Rooftop Leaders who are committed to building strategic movements inside their arena. You will learn the same advanced methods Scott learned as a Green Beret, strategic communicator, and influencer to find your vision for a better life and business and inspire others to help you build it. You will join a growing, elite tribe of leaders from all disciplines and walks of life who are bound by one common idea: moving the people around you to action like never before. It's not for everybody, but if you think you have what it takes to be part of our executive coaching program, go to www.scottmann.com to learn more or reach out to us here: info@scottmann.com.

Executive Consulting

Do you face wicked, complex problems as a business owner, executive, or entrepreneur? Do you feel like you're the only person on the planet awake at night as you wrestle with the heavy load that only executives and business owners understand? Scott has been strategically advising and consulting senior leaders on navigating wicked problems for decades. His tailored peer-to-peer approach to navigating complexity and leading when it's hard have empowered Fortune 500 CEOs and small and medium-size business owners. Scott's tailored approach to consulting will not only arm you with a competitive edge in how you take on thorny, executive-level problems but will also provide you a thought partner and battle buddy to help you step through the toughest of situations. If you'd like to schedule a discovery call or discussion with Scott about his consulting services, go to www.scottmann.com to learn more or reach out to us here: info@scottmann.com.

LGOCF ECOSYSTEM

You are not alone!

With the Churn all around us, it's easy to feel you have to fight back by yourself.

Well, I'm here to tell you in no uncertain terms, that's not true.

In my book *Game Changers*, I related the story of how US paratroopers led the 1944 Allied invasion of Europe by parachuting into Nazi-occupied France. Invariably these paratroopers became scattered because of winds, darkness, confusion, and enemy forces.

Surely, they felt alone and isolated while searching for their comrades behind enemy lines, but senior leadership anticipated this and equipped each paratrooper with a small device that when pressed made the sound of a cricket.

As each paratrooper moved through the dangerous hedgerows infested with German machine-gun nests, they would carefully initiate their cricket device, which would be answered by another cricket device in the near distance. One by one, two by two, these airborne soldiers would find each other in the darkness to form LGOPS (Little Groups of Paratroopers). Through recognizable sounds in the darkness, these LGOPS formed powerful ecosystems that organically gathered power to make a stand.

Today, you and I face a different enemy—the Churn—but you don't have to do it alone. We can create our own ecosystem. Let's call it the *LGOCFs—Little Groups of Churn Fighters*!

Within the swirling Churn, there are bottom-up leaders and organizations who are sounding off with their cricket devices. They aren't waiting for permission from the divisionists. Instead, they are carving out change and chirping in the darkness for the rest of us to find our way to them.

I compiled this list below to serve as a point of departure to make your own LGOCF connections, to help you navigate the Churn, leverage the human operating system, find deep meaning in your life, and connect as if your life depends on it.

It's by no means inclusive, but it's a damn good start.

1. The Conciliators Guild

Why you should care: They leverage new knowledge to widen context in politics, help increase tolerance and nimbleness of mind, and encourage the development of practical solutions.

Scott's endorsement: Their workshops and innovative

projects give you a competitive edge in how you engage others, no matter what your industry or profession.

www.conciliators-guild.org

2. Braver Angels

Why you should care: They are the nation's largest bipartisan, volunteer-led movement to bridge the partisan divide.

Scott's endorsement: Through community gatherings, real debates, and grassroots leaders working together, they are creating hope and showing Americans a better way out of the Churn.

https://braverangels.org

3. More in Common

Why you should care: They will expose you to the potential strength of the "exhausted majority."

Scott's endorsement: This organization recognizes that the forces of division are driving societies apart. They bring in groundbreaking research and solutions to drive social change at scale. I strongly recommend the "Hidden Tribes of America" project.

www.moreincommon.com

4. Tristan Harris and Aza Raskin

Why you should care: They take an in-depth look at the risk that AI poses to a functional society.

Scott's endorsement: These thought leaders are breaking new ground on what the technology race of the attention-based economy means to how we live our lives. I also recommend their seminal video *The Social Dilemma*.

www.youtube.com/watch?v=cB0_-qKbal4

5. Lucas Miller and Dr. Sahar Yousef

Why you should care: They illuminate how distractions from our mobile devices are the number one threat to high performance.

Scott's endorsement: They have done amazing work on framing the negative impact that smartphones and other aspects of technology can have on our ancient brains. Equally important, they have created simple and powerful tools to optimize high performance and move from becoming a passenger to a driver in the use of technology.

www.becomingsuperhuman.science

6. Jim VandeHei and Mike Allen

Why you should care: We've been deceived into thinking we are more divided, dysfunctional, and more defeated than we actually are.

Scott's endorsement: "Behind the Curtain" is a powerful article in Axios that shows how the fringe "divisionists" are exploiting the exhausted majority and what we can do to reclaim our collective agency.

www.axios.com/2024/04/09/america-politics-divided-polarization-data

7. Joe Griffin and Ivan Tyrrell

Why you should care: They provide unprecedented understanding of the human operating system and components of getting MESSSy.

Scott's endorsement: If you ever wondered what makes us tick, this body of work is for you. It's essential as a baseline for navigating the engagements in your life. I strongly recommend the book *The Human Givens* and the Human Givens Institute.

www.humangivens.com

8. Iain McGilchrist

Why you should care: He'll help you understand our ancient brain in the context of the modern Churn and "how to get without getting got!"

Scott's endorsement: This TED Talk efficiently helps you gain an understanding of the divided brain by explaining why our modern tendencies are moving us toward a more disconnected state from ourselves and the natural world. It's foundational for taking on the Churn.

www.ted.com/talks/iain_mcgilchrist_the_divided_brain

9. Jared Diamond

Why you should care: He provides commonsense insights for understanding our primal nature in the modern world.

Scott's endorsement: Jared Diamond's *The World Until Yesterday* is one of the best below-the-waterline assets I've come across. He really helps you understand why we are far more traditional than we are modern.

www.jareddiamond.org/Jared_Diamond/My_Books.html

10. Sebastian Junger

Why you should care: He offers great insights into the power of community in times of low trust.

Scott's endorsement: Junger's research into communal and tribal realities has a ton of practical applications for our modern world as well as some serious cautions about the growth of contempt in our time of Churn.

www.sebastianjunger.com

11. Jonathan Haidt

Why you should care: He takes an unapologetic and revealing look at social media and its negative impacts on our civil society.

Scott's endorsement: While published on a subscription-based platform, the article linked below is a definite must-read for mapping out the Churn. Haidt has also done significant research on identifying groups like More in Common that are taking a stand against "divisionist" leaders.

www.theatlantic.com/magazine/archive/2022/05 /social-media-democracy-trust-babel/629369

12. Matthew Lieberman

Why you should care: He unpacks the social component of getting MESSSy.

Scott's endorsement: Lieberman will help you understand why humans being social is our superpower. His book *Social* is outstanding, as is his TEDx.

www.penguinrandomhouse.com/authors/176947 /matthew-d-lieberman

13. Viktor Frankl

Why you should care: Frankl provides a timeless perspective on the importance of integrating meaning in all that we do.

Scott's endorsement: I strongly recommend his book *Man's Search for Meaning* as a primer for purpose integration into your leadership body of work.

www.viktorfranklinstitute.org/publications

14. Bo Eason

Why you should care: He elucidates the physicality of storytelling.

Scott's endorsement: Bo's book *There's No Plan B for Your A-Game* and his Personal Power Story Events are incredibly helpful to your narrative competence training.

https://boeason.com

15. Kendall Haven

Why you should care: He provides the best insights on the science of storytelling.

Scott's endorsement: I recommend the books *Story Proof* and *Story Smart* as essential reads for upping your storytelling game. You can also check out my interview with him on *The Rooftop Podcast*.

www.kendallhaven.com

16. Robert Putnam

Why you should care: He paints a vision beyond the Churn and illuminates the science of human connection.

Scott's endorsement: Putnam's books *Bowling Alone* and *The Upswing* have helped me frame a vision for better days that I believe is available to us as a positive alternative to the Churn.

http://robertdputnam.com

17. Ori Brafman and Rod Beckstrom

Why you should care: They demonstrate the power of getting big sh*t done from the bottom up.

Scott's endorsement: If you feel an affinity to the chapter in this book on connection and communities of practice, I strongly recommend their book *The Starfish and the Spider*.

www.penguinrandomhouse.com/books/298214/the-starfish
-and-the-spider-by-ori-brafman-and-rod-a-beckstrom

18. Steven Pressfield

Why you should care: He shows an excellent understanding of how self-sabotage (Resistance) feeds the Churn.

Scott's endorsement: You can't go wrong with Steve's books. For starters, pick up *The War of Art* and *Turning Pro*. You'll get excellent insights into Resistance, as well as ways to overcome it in daily life. Steve also provides helpful insights into status behavior and the power of tribe.

https://stevenpressfield.com/home

19. Ben and Jess Owen

Why you should care: They demonstrate the bottom-up community of practice in action.

Scott's endorsement: I highly recommend my *Rooftop Podcast* interview with Ben Owen. If you want to contribute to the upswing, their foundation is a damn good place to do it. I also recommend following them on LinkedIn if you want to learn how to be a "Verizon Guy" strategic catalyst.

https://wefightmonsters.org

20. Joseph Campbell

Why you should care: He is the master of the Hero's Journey framework.

Scott's endorsement: His book *The Hero with a Thousand Faces* will help you get your head around the origins and the framework of the Hero's Journey for designing compelling narratives.

www.jcf.org/about-joseph-campbell-foundation

21. Jean-Louis Rodrigue

Why you should care: He is a master of the physicality of delivering powerful stories and speeches.

Scott's endorsement: If you want to level up your ability to connect deeply and influence authentically, Jean-Louis's "Back to the Body" is not just a tool for actors, but for anyone who must engage as a speaker or presenter.

https://alexandertechworks.com/video_category/jean-louis-rodrigue

22. Daniel Coyle

Why you should care: He helps us understand the "biological necessity" of struggle, along with the culture of purpose and connection.

Scott's endorsement: Coyle has written two incredible works, *The Little Book of Talent* and *The Culture Code*. They are essential reads for Rooftop Leadership.

https://danielcoyle.com

23. Warren Berger

Why you should care: He is a "questionologist" who will help you ask more beautiful questions.

Scott's endorsement: *The Book of Beautiful Questions* is an outstanding resource for improving your daily skill at human engagement. You can also listen to Warren's interview with me on *The Rooftop Podcast.*

https://warrenberger.com

24. Romy and Gaby Camargo

Why you should care: Their story will show you the power of meaning in the toughest of situations.

Scott's endorsement: If you want to contribute to the upswing, their rehabilitation center is a damn good place to do it. I also recommend a visit to Stay In Step if you are ever in the Tampa Bay area and want to see a real-life inspiration for getting big sh*t done.

https://stayinstep.org

25. Jesse Torgerson

Why you should care: She teaches you how to use breath to reduce tension in the body and be more influential.

Scott's endorsement: I have worked with Jesse for years while training as a speaker and actor. She traveled with our cast to every *Last Out* tour stop in 2023 and helped our combat veteran cast metabolize anxiety and trauma to give the best possible performances. She can help you as a corporate leader, sales professional, or speaker. Her sessions are in-person or via Zoom.

https://jessetorgerson.com

26. Belisa Vranich

Why you should care: She shows you how to unlock your breathing for high performance.

Scott's endorsement: You must read *Breathing for Warriors*. Dr. Vranich, a psychologist and breathing expert, will help you optimize your breathing to focus your inner game and perform at the highest level in everything from Ultimate Fighting to keynotes to sales pitches. She can also train and certify breath coaches to spread this dynamic capability within your organization.

www.thebreathingclass.com

27. Michael Davis

Why you should care: The "Story Doctor" will help you design the most impactful story.

Scott's endorsement: Michael understands story structure and design better than anyone I've ever worked with. If you are putting a talk or presentation together, he's your guy. He's also a wonderful TEDx coach. And if you are looking for help with framing or putting a hard topic into words for a title, there is no one better.

https://speakingcpr.com

28. Jason Cannon

Why you should care: He is an expert on the integration of designing and delivering powerful stories.

Scott's endorsement: As a playwright, actor, and speaker coach, Jason can help you build strong practices for storytelling preparation. He can also help you craft and integrate powerful speeches and presentations. If you are looking to publish your story, I also recommend him. His book *This Above All* is just top-notch for living a creative and artistic life. I believe in it so much I wrote the foreword.

https://jasoncannon.art

29. Jerry Lujan

Why you should care: He can help you get clear on your why and find the best use of your energy to lead.

Scott's endorsement: Jerry is one of the best "bottom-up" leaders I've ever been around. If you look up *grind* in the dictionary, you'll find his photo. He and his team are experts at helping people find clarity when they are stuck. His programs can promote self-awareness of you and your team, allowing you to elevate and grow. This guy knows how to infuse purpose into everything you do and gain four times the impact as a result.

https://elevation180.com

30. David Martin

Why you should care: He can teach to harness your "inner genius" to get big sh*t done.

Scott's endorsement: David has been coaching high performers for decades. He coaches me. David's book *Free the Genius* is an inspirational read for anyone pursuing strategic objectives. If you are feeling like there is a bigger game you should be playing, then a visit to David's "Genius Farm" in Cincinnati for one-on-one coaching can help you get to the clarity of purpose we all need for impact in the Churn.

https://davidmartinco.com/free-the-genius-free-your-genius

31. Randall Surles

Why you should care: He can help you birth your scar story into a powerful book.

Scott's endorsement: Every emerging author should have an editor and thought partner they can trust. Randy is a former Green Beret with unmatched skills in designing stories that work. For veterans looking to tell their story, Randy has your back.

www.militaryeditor.com

ABOUT THE AUTHOR

 Lt. Col. Scott Mann is a retired Green Beret with over twenty-two years of Army and special operations experience around the world, and a *New York Times* bestselling author. He has deployed to Ecuador, Colombia, Peru, Iraq, and Afghanistan. He is the CEO of Rooftop Leadership and the founder of a 501(c)(3), The Heroes Journey, committed to helping veterans tell their stories in transition. Scott regularly speaks to and trains corporate leaders, law enforcement, and special operations forces on best practices for going local, storytelling, and making better human connections. Scott has made frequent appearances on Fox News, CNN, and other national platforms as a thought leader on building organizational relationships, restoring trust in our communities, and a range of national security issues. He is also an actor and playwright who has written a play about the US

war in Afghanistan called *Last Out: Elegy of a Green Beret* on Amazon Prime. Scott lives in Florida with his wife, Monty, where they are deepening their skills on empty nesting.

If you'd like to have Scott Mann speak at your next event or if you are interested in any of Scott's body of work with leadership, veteran advocacy, or storytelling, go to scottmann.com to learn more.